THE GOLDEN BOOK OF HU

ALSO BY MICHAEL AVERY

The Secret Language of Waking Dreams

THE GOLDEN BOOK OF HU

Michael and Pichaya Avery

Susan Creek Books
Wilsonville, Oregon

Available through Amazon
Also, please see authors' blog at:
https://signssynchronicityandwakingdreams.com

The Golden Book of HU

Copyright © 2024 Michael and Pichaya Avery

Cover design by Michael Avery
Graphics by Michael Avery and Claude Gruffy
Initial edit by Karla Joy McMechan
Typeset by Rose Elphick

ISBN: 978-0-9748716-5-3
Library of Congress Control Number: 2024911664

For those seeking permission to reproduce material credited to sources listed in the Notes section, please direct your requests to the original authors who hold those copyrights. Please feel free to use and pass on the insights and tools listed in this book with proper credit.

This book is a reflection of the authors' and various contributors' own spiritual understandings and is not intended to speak for any spiritual path, teacher, or religion. In certain places, references are made to Eckankar and adepts associated with that teaching. We have intended only to make 'fair use' of any trademarked terms; this does not imply endorsement or sponsorship by that organization or any other.

The information presented here—as with any outside information—should be viewed as seed material for contemplation only.

Dedication

To the Voice of HU

Table of Contents

Preface: Dreams of a Golden Book ix
Introduction xiii

PART I: CONNECTING WITH THE VOICE OF HU

1) The Sanctuary of HU 3
2) *A Cosmic Sea of Words* 17
3) Dreams and the Dream Teacher 29
4) The Himalayan Temple 41

PART II: SOLVING LIFE'S CHALLENGES WITH HU

5) Through the Doors of HU and Other Spiritual Exercises 57
6) In Search of True North: Healing with HU 71
7) Opening the Heart with HU 85
8) Being HU 97

PART III: THE UNIVERSE *IS* HU

9) The Many Miracles of HU 113
10) Animals Love HU, Too 127
11) Sharing the Gift of HU 139
12) Love Is a Never-ending Story 149

Epilogue: The Sound of Spiritual Freedom 163
Acknowledgments 167
Notes 169

Preface:
Dreams of a Golden Book

When my wife, Pichaya (PEACH-a-ya), and I first began our tradition of sharing our nightly dreams and insights at the breakfast table each morning before dawn, we didn't think of it as a spiritual exercise. However, "Coffee with Honey," as we affectionately called it, was just that. As our diets changed, so did the name. We decided to call it "Conversations with Honey."

Oi, Pichaya's nickname (which rhymes with "Joy"), suggested that we start each morning by singing *HU*, a sacred song of love. This is to align ourselves with Divine Spirit and set the tone for the day.

While my contributions usually revolve around insights, one morning I shared a recurring dream that I'd found captivating. In the dream, I was shown a beautiful golden book that Oi and I had written together. This was perplexing, since we hadn't written a book like this and had no plans to do so.

Oi listened politely in silence until I had finished. "Recently, I had a dream about a book surrounded by a golden glow," she commented. "I wonder if our dreams are related."

Oi's journal entry, dated July 1, 2021, gives further details about her prophetic dream.

I was escorted by a spiritual teacher to a Temple of Golden Wisdom[1] where I was shown an illuminated book resting on a pedestal. The powerful golden glow radiating from the book took my breath away. As I drew closer, I noticed something puzzling. There was no title, only Mike's and my names on the cover.

"When I tune into our book in my dream," I told her, "it has a golden glow around it, too. I wonder what the book is about." During our Conversations with Honey each morning, we discussed many fascinating possibilities for the mysterious golden book. Nothing seemed to fit.

Then, on Christmas Day of 2021, I opened the gift Oi had given me and, lo and behold, there was our answer, although we didn't recognize it then. I held in my hands a brand new HU song CD.[2] On it, a spiritual exercise called "The Doors of HU" was described.

Following the instructions that evening, Oi and I each imagined ourselves standing before the two doors of HU. In my imagination, I opened the wooden door marked *H*, while Oi opened the *U* door to its right. We walked into a spacious sanctuary together. Upon completing the exercise, we compared notes and found that, once inside the sanctuary, we had viewed a similar scene. Apparently, we had been given a special gift, a glimpse of the book we had seen in our dreams, one we presumably were supposed to write.

Oi turned to me and said, "I think it is a book about HU."

"There must be hundreds of references to the word *HU*," I observed. HU has been known by various cultures and religions throughout history. What could we possibly add to that?"

"We can contemplate on it," Oi suggested.

Surprisingly, the next morning I awoke with a handful of working chapter titles that partially answered my question. This gave us more seeds for contemplation, but I still had my doubts.

Oi and I then drove to the river where we feed jays, squirrels, some year-round ducks, and Shadow, the resident grey cat. Near the boat ramp, we noticed twelve electric-blue, star-shaped balloons at the base of an Oak tree. We looked upon this unusual event as a waking dream, an outer event connected to an inner process.[3] In this case, our attention was focused on "the golden book."

We interpreted seeing the twelve balloons to mean that our prospective book, should we choose to write it, would have twelve chapters. When a beautiful rainbow—our confirmation symbol—appeared in the dark blue sky as we were leaving the river, we made the decision to begin the project and pointed our car toward an unknown destination.

Please note that the primary voice in this book is mine. Oi's stories are identified along the way.

—Mike and Oi

Introduction

Writing brings us joy, not only because we find satisfaction in putting words down on paper, but also due to the love we feel flowing through us when we tune in to the "celestial music." This symphony of the universe begins and ends with *HU*, the original sound that created Soul in this universe as well as the myriad worlds. Each Soul adds Its own unique "electronic keynote," also known as its *resonance signature*, to the chorus of the universe. The melding of all keynotes in creation can be heard as *HU*, the most sacred of all sounds.

HU is recognized as the true name of the Creator by spiritual travelers who have explored the highest dimensions of life. It is also said to be an ancient name for God. The etymology of the word *God*, also used for the Creator, can be traced back to *HU* as the name people use to call upon God.[1] *HU* is actually the Voice of God, the sound that comes from the Infinite Ocean of Love beyond all worlds.

This high consciousness of HU in motion is also known as Divine Spirit, the Holy Spirit, the Sound Current, or Audible Life Stream, to name a few. There are also many titles assigned to those holding this high state of consciousness, including the Mahanta, the Wayshower, the Inner Teacher, the Sat Guru, the Beloved, the Light Giver, and the Vi-Guru. Each name or title is an attempt at expressing in words the essence of HU: divine love.

Regardless of religion or creed, divine love will appear in any form familiar to us. Spirit, HU in motion, fills the mold we extend with our thoughts, beliefs, and imagination.

In this book, the term "Inner Teacher" is most often used to describe the highest expression of the Creator. Singing *HU* connects us directly to this high consciousness of love.

Many of those we've spoken with over the years have sung *HU* while requesting assistance, as have we. Asking for help, after we've done all we can, is a form of self-love. It is understood that we don't sing *HU* to change another's beliefs, health, or life experience. Sending love through the vibration of HU, however, opens the door for the Divine to assist in any way It deems appropriate.

Once I realized, with Oi's help, that it's all about love, I discovered the greatest benefit from singing *HU*: to fully open our heart to God's love. Those who approach the Inner Teacher asking to be connected to the Light and Sound of Spirit are never turned away, regardless of the individual's motive or state of consciousness. By practicing contemplative exercises and singing *HU*, he or she will one day request of the Divine, "Please show me love."

Giving and receiving love at our deepest, most intimate, level is both joyous and effortless. But here in the physical world, emotional scars, crippling judgments, and outdated beliefs, keep us from enjoying this ebb and flow of love. By listening to the inner sounds of the Audible Life Stream and singing *HU*, we can lift our consciousness and gradually transcend all self-created limitations. This includes what we sometimes call "karma," those actions from our past waiting to be balanced as their lessons are learned.

Introduction

Reviewing what I'd written thus far, I gave myself a measured nod of approval. After all, self-love is an important key to maintaining a connection with Divine Spirit. Solid spiritual foundations are built upon self-awareness, self-love, and self-responsibility. However, I also realized that everything I had stated regarding HU has been spoken about or written before. While I was confident that Oi and I would receive insights and divine guidance, I was still skeptical.

Then, quite unexpectedly, words carrying a familiar tone began to form in my consciousness, reminding me of softly falling snow. A memorable scene from my youth came to mind, a winter morning when I'd been out in the woods alone searching for a Christmas tree.

"Why don't you write a book that *you'd* enjoy reading?" the Inner Teacher suggested. "I'll send help your way to 'decorate the tree.'"

And so, the golden book became our primary focus each morning during Conversations with Honey. We had no working title and no specific direction, only trust in the Inner Teacher who immediately sent help our way. As chronicled in Chapter One, it came from an unexpected source. By the time we had finished the book, Oi and I had gained an even greater appreciation for the Inner Teacher and the way Divine Spirit works in our lives.

Part I
Connecting with the Voice of HU

- 1 -

THE SANCTUARY OF HU

*"He is the First, He is the Last.
He is the Outward, He is the Inward.
I know of nothing but Hu, none but Him."*

—Rumi
Love is a Stranger[1]

Tossing the roadmap aside, I set off excitedly down the highway ready to embrace the Inner Teacher's suggestion about writing a book that I'd enjoy reading. *Are there really any roads less traveled yet to be explored regarding HU?* I wondered. Honestly, I didn't know. Only the Inner Teacher knew and, so far, our trusted guide was silent.

Now what?" I asked myself, as, once again, Oi and I were pulling out of the parking lot at the river where we feed peanuts to the jays and squirrels. Oi sat beside me, silently, her eyes closed, contemplating on our earlier discussion at the park about the possible contents of our golden book. My mind was blank—so much for writing anything unique about HU. I smiled at my presumptuousness. Had I really expected words to magically pop into my mind from out of the blue?

Then, surprisingly, less than five minutes later, I became aware of a subtle string of words bubbling up from an inner well. I shifted more of my attention away from the road signs and passing cars to this dream-like dialogue happening within. *Does it make sense?* I asked myself.

Yes, it does, came the answer. And, I heard the word *HU* mentioned in what appeared to be an inner discourse. Help had arrived from the Inner Teacher in an unexpected way.

The Sanctuary

Speaking matter-of-factly, this unidentified voice was describing a sacred place on the inner planes:

In the Temple of Param Akshar on the Soul Plane, there is a sanctuary, the Sanctuary of HU. This sanctuary is accessed through two massive wooden doors at its entrance. The letter H is carved on the left door; the right one bears the letter U.

Resting upon a pedestal of living gold in the center of the semi-circular auditorium is a book, The Golden Book of HU. This sanctuary is more than a building within the greater temple where Souls gather to soak in the love of the Creator and learn the history of the universe. It is a place of power where the Infinite kneels beside the altar of the finite.

One might think these sacred grounds would be reserved for those Souls whom you call "masters" or perhaps the highest of initiates, but this is not the case. Kindness, honesty, and a love of truth are the only keys needed to arrive at any of the temple gates. First-time visitors will be asked in whose name they have come and to speak the name of the Living Word; upon doing this, entrance is granted. Subsequent visits will not require this formality. To enter the Sanctuary of HU directly, bypassing the temple gates, simply sing the name of the Living Word with love and imagine yourself walking through the double doors of the sanctuary with the Inner Teacher.

Within these hallowed temple grounds, numerous footpaths wind their way through exotic gardens of aromatic flora, vast forest greenery, and singing, healing waters. Peace and tranquility refresh all who come here to the Temple of Param Akshar. Now, be at peace.

The brief communication ended, leaving me staring blankly in silence at the oncoming traffic. I glanced over at Oi. She was sound asleep in the passenger seat beside me, unaware that anything out of the ordinary had happened. I replayed the message in my mind in order to commit to memory what I had heard as accurately as possible. *What was the source of this information?* I wondered. *Would I ever hear from it again?*

Upon arriving home, I raced for the computer and drafted the beginning of Chapter One. Since Oi was in the final stages of her own project, I chose to keep my excitement about starting a new book to myself. However, over dinner, I shared some of these revelations and how I believed that our dreams about writing a golden book were connected to The Golden Book of HU.

Later that night, I followed the instructions I'd been given on how to visit Param Akshar. I let my consciousness reach out until I found the doors of the Sanctuary. While listening to the inner voice earlier, it had been necessary to dedicate much of my attention to driving. This time was different. Directly in front of me glistened the golden pedestal upon which rested The Golden Book of HU. This was my first close-up look at one of the greatest treasures of the ages. It was electrifying, breathtaking, majestic—it was magnificent.

When I shifted my attention to the field of energy surrounding the book, I felt an inexplicable sense of wonder and awe envelop me. There was a powerful presence gazing back at me from this spherical field of energy; or perhaps it was the sphere itself that was alive. I yearned to know more.

I drank in as many details as I could absorb. There was love, tranquility, grandeur, and the sacredness of this ancient place. I imagined all the fortunate Souls who had stood where I was now standing, wondering if their experience was anything as life changing as mine.

Returning to normal waking consciousness, I basked in the lingering afterglow of my discovery. On this initial visit, upon my arrival, I had been greeted by a "welcoming presence." I sensed it was the being who occupied the sphere around The Golden Book. Several questions came to mind and begged to be answered. But it was the love I had experienced that called to my heart. "Come back to Param Akshar," it beckoned.

* * *

I drew in a deep breath, exhaled, and read through what I had written about the Sanctuary of HU. Inwardly, I heard the soft voice of the Inner Teacher.

"Unique enough for you?" he questioned.

"It was totally unexpected," I answered. "Thank you for giving me this profound experience. I'm honored and appreciative." I imagined a playful smile beaming back at me.

As my interest in proceeding with our project blossomed, I looked forward to my contemplations and spiritual exercises again. I was fascinated by The Golden Book and had many questions. More startling information came through on my second visit, as described in a journal entry:

Mike's Journal, March 27, 2022

I approach the radiant book. It is bright, but not too bright. A deep feeling of peace washes through me. All worldly cares and distractions are beginning to fade. They are but distant memories, unreal, unimportant, aside from the lessons they have provided. I feel loved in this room and feel love pouring from my heart to all of creation. I wonder to myself if this is what is meant by "resting in the arms of the Divine."

I understand that the sanctuary at Param Akshar is secretly called the "House of the Living Word." I'm taken aback when I realize that I am communicating with this Living Word, and it is the source of the earlier discourse as Oi and I were leaving the river. The "Voice of HU," as I began calling it, knows me by my *Soul keynote*. I recognize the keynote of the Creator flowing through the light surrounding The Golden Book and hear beautiful music.

Information about my individuality in this universe is opening before my consciousness. I receive another shock: I existed *before* coming into this universe. In fact, I have always existed. The creation of my Soul body by the Creator was necessary in order for me to participate in this universe, experiencing limitation and individuality.

"What was I before coming here?" I question. The Voice of HU answers:

"Like all others, you were, are, and always will be, a drop from the Infinite Ocean of Love. You, and your fellow travelers, are emissaries of the Divine, entrusted with the expansion of creation. The Ocean is in the drop as the

drop is in the Ocean. All are one, so to speak, yet all are individual. It is a concept beyond the ability of the mind to comprehend.

"In the true realm of reality, there is no one being, nor is there a realm, nor is there such a thing as reality. To be real would presuppose that something unreal exists, which it does not. You have always existed in an eternal state beyond being and non-being. The Infinite Ocean of Love is a descriptive appellation representing That Which Is, the Allness without division or description."

I ask about my highest purpose as Soul. The Voice of HU responds:

"You are here to experience the wonders of polarity—the adventures, the mysteries, the dramas, and discoveries, the lessons to be learned in an environment of such extremes. Poetically, you have come here to dance with creation. First and foremost, your highest purpose is to find new ways to express more bountifully the love that you are."

"What is the significance of The Golden Book?" I ask. Familiar images from my early twenties appear before my vision.

A co-worker and I are *en route* to the Grand Canyon. We've been laid off from the plywood mill where we work due to rising veneer costs. I am recording my thoughts, observations, and memorable experiences from this impromptu vacation in a comprehensive journal.

Through these images, the Voice of HU is implying that The Golden Book is an all-inclusive, interactive "cosmic journal." The book appears to contain a historical record of everything in the Creator's universe. This includes all that It deems important, interesting, and noteworthy as seen through Its own eyes and experienced by Souls in Its myriad worlds.

As my contemplation ended, I heard a faint impression echo through the recesses of my mind. It had originated in the Sanctuary of HU: *"Now, Beloved one, be at peace."*

* * *

On at least one occasion, I have found myself at a temple beyond this physical world standing before another inner book. No words were written on its pages. The information was transferred through the light radiating from the book. With The Golden Book of HU, however, even from a distance, I learned that my questions can be answered through direct communication with the soothing, yet powerful, voice emanating from the sphere of influence surrounding the book.

On subsequent visits to the sanctuary, I could see words forming on the pages of the book when the Voice of HU spoke. As the pages turned, those words vanished like morning mist on a summer's day. On rare occasions, I experienced downloads of knowingness comprised of images and emotions. But, for the most part, I only heard the Voice. If you replay in your mind a recent conversation you've had with a friend, you will better understand the texture of these communications.

* * *

A true spiritual adept has the ability to teach in the physical realm as well as operate in the spiritual worlds. The primary role of the Inner Teacher is that of a wayshower. He has the authority to guide Soul on Its way back through the worlds of duality into the Fifth Plane and beyond.

I have learned that it never hurts to ask. When in doubt about anything, I contact the Inner Teacher who will gladly answer questions and provide guidance as long as it is in the best interest of all. Many are taught through dreams or waking dreams while others may develop clear inner communication.

It's understandable that some readers might question the reality of such experiences as speaking inwardly with a spiritual guide or visits in consciousness to other dimensions. When I was in my twenties, I harbored doubts of my own. These centered around the reality and protection of the Inner Teacher and Divine Spirit. But after a memorable morning on the shores of Oahu, all doubts vanished. From that point forward, perhaps because I had shifted from belief into knowingness, the inner channels of communication slowly began to open up.

Turning Points

Blue Star over Waikiki

At the age of twenty-eight, I moved to Honolulu where I lived for the better part of a year behind the International Marketplace in Waikiki. Seven years had passed since I'd read my first book on out-of-the-body travel, *The Tiger's Fang*, by Paul Twitchell. I was about to learn more.

When some friends came to visit from Oregon, we packed a lunch and some towels, then headed straight for the beach. After renting surfboards from a stand in front of the Royal Hawaiian Hotel, we swam out to catch some waves. It was a memorable morning. Just before noon, my friends called it a day and waved for me to join them on the beach for lunch. Instead, I paddled out for one last ride.

Instead of resting after the tiresome swim out, I took my place at the end of a row of locals straddling their personalized surfboards. A glance over my shoulder in the direction of the open sea confirmed what the other surfers already knew—a big wave was building. I paddled ahead furiously, catching the wave along with the locals. I was on top of the world.

My feeling of exhilaration vanished, however, when I tumbled off the back of my board. As I bobbed up and down in the tropical surf, I watched the other riders cruise in to shore fifty yards away. I could see my rented board floating in their midst. Heaving a weary sigh, I started the long swim back. It took only a moment to realize my terrible predicament.

My arms felt like lead. I swam five difficult yards, then went under. I called out, but the pounding surf drowned my cries for help. Again, I went under. Only this time when I surfaced, I popped right out of my body.

What a startling experience! I was simply a viewpoint. With heightened clarity and surprising calmness, I surveyed my grim situation from a vantage point about three feet above my left shoulder. I felt no fear, nor was there a sense of desperation or urgency. Mostly, I was mesmerized by the variety of bright colors: the swimsuits, the towels, the flamingo-pink face of the Royal Hawaiian Hotel. My own towel was spread out in front of the Outrigger next door. *Will I ever lie on it again?* I wondered, without concern. Laughing children splashed in the water near the edge of the surf. An indescribable feeling of joy permeated the atmosphere.

There was no perception of time, nor was I particularly attached to the outcome of the drama. I was merely an observer. In fact, as I reveled in this remarkable new freedom, the probability that I would leave the body permanently within the next few minutes seemed far less important than fully processing my new insight: that I exist, independent of the body, as a spiritual being.

My second insight was as unexpected as the first. Suddenly, I returned to the body. Another huge wave towered above me. In that moment, my heart sank as I faced the inevitable. There was no way out. Only then did I remember to call on the Inner Teacher for help. I was barely able to whisper a quick, impassioned plea.

As the wave crashed over me, I threw out my arms in desperation. A dull thud sent vibrations reverberating up my right arm. I'd hit a board. I held to it with all my strength as it drifted gently toward shore. I was too weak to pull myself on top, so I clung to it thankfully, resting my head on its surface. A warm wave of relief flooded through me when my toes finally touched sand. Slowly, I opened my eyes and looked around. How could I thank the board's owner?

But no one appeared to be searching for a missing board. With growing perplexity, I scanned the beach, this time in a 360-degree sweep. Then, I happened to glance down at the board. I stared at the number "15" in stunned disbelief. It was the same one I had rented only four hours earlier.

That night, I posed for a picture with my friends from the mainland on a narrow lanai overlooking Waikiki. I was the one with the biggest smile. When the prints came back, I noticed something unusual. Above my right shoulder, where a distant light had refracted in the camera lens, shone a blue-white light in the form of a star. It was a message from the Inner Teacher, a confirmation of divine intervention, what I would later call a "waking dream."

This proved to be a turning point in my life. I came away from my near-death experience with two powerful insights: I was more than a physical body, and help was available for the asking. I had experienced the real me, call it Soul if you will, and I knew that no matter what happened in my life after that, "I always will BE."

At times, Divine Spirit will intervene even without our asking. Oi experienced this during one of the most challenging times in her life. Thankfully, she had developed the awareness to recognize the guidance of the Inner Teacher.

I Am Loved Beyond Measure by Pichaya (Oi)

"What is my purpose for living?" I asked the Inner Teacher during an intense dark night of the Soul. I was in my early forties, living in a luxurious feathered nest with my precious family, yet I was unhappy. As a housewife and a mother of three, I often felt unworthy, unappreciated, and unloved. My heart yearned to become something more.

For several years, I had been chronically depressed and developed a serious eating disorder called bulimia, characterized by a destructive cycle of binging large amounts of food and purging through fasting and excessive exercise. It was potentially life-threatening, but I did not seek professional help. Intuitively, I knew I could heal myself with the Inner Teacher's guidance. I read hundreds of self-help books and practiced my spiritual exercises faithfully. Even then, the dark night of the Soul was so excruciating that I decided to end my life.

One freezing cold morning while making a cup of coffee, I thought about the specific way I would commit suicide and told myself, "Today is the day. Life can go on without me. I am ready."

Then, I heard the Inner Teacher speak to me firmly, loudly, and clearly: "Go to your contemplation room, pick up a book, and open it at random," he directed. With complete obedience, I walked into the room, removed a book from the shelf, opened it, and read these words: "Life is worth living."

My Teacher spoke compassionately, "I love you. You need to learn to love yourself."

Before I knew it, I found myself sobbing uncontrollably on the floor. The powerful presence of the Divine filled the void in my heart. I felt an immediate shift in my awareness as feelings of depression were transmuted by the Teacher's love. I then realized that he had answered my question, "What is my purpose for living?" The answer is: to learn how to love, which begins with loving myself the way my Teacher loves me.

This profound experience was a major turning point in my life. It deepened my relationship with the Inner Teacher and enhanced my awareness of how Divine Spirit speaks. The passage in the book—"Life is worth living"—reminded me of my favorite quote about love: "Soul exists because God loves It."[2] The Inner Teacher's love has transformed my life and inspires me to extend his love to others who face loneliness, heartache, and despair.

*   *   *

During our initial conversations about writing this book, I voiced to Oi and wondered to myself, *Why me? What makes me any kind of an authority on HU?* I had read very few books of late, due in part to eyesight challenges, and my schedule for practicing my contemplative exercises was erratic at times. Oi, however, was just the opposite. She was extremely disciplined. She got up each morning at 2:00 a.m. to sing *HU* and write.

Then, a rather comical, yet painfully accurate, answer came. An image appeared in my imagination as we were driving to the river one afternoon. It was a tight-rope walker wrapped in bandages from head to toe. Besides the scrapes, I sensed that he had broken most of the bones in his body from previous falls while performing without a net. Yet, here he was, once again climbing the ladder to the high wire.

What a curious image, I thought to myself. I was startled when I heard the Voice from the Sanctuary forming words within my consciousness:

"You were chosen for this project because you've always done things a bit differently. Since you read very little, you are more or less a clean slate. To your credit, you've earned the trust of the Inner Teacher, as has Oi.

"You have firsthand knowledge about the reality of HU and the Inner Teacher. It is true that knowing about the path is not the same as knowing the path. The vibration of knowingness resonates from the space behind written words garnered from personal experience. In going forward, you need only walk the path with a heart for service and conduct your life in a more disciplined manner, fitting for a higher Soul.

"You could view your role in this project as a writer and transcriber. Oi has insights which make her a perfect complement and can testify to the benefits of singing HU. Her decision to set her own book aside and focus on this one says a lot about her. Now, be at peace."

- 2 -

A Cosmic Sea of Words

"The Supreme Being has been called by various names in different languages, but the mystics have known his as Hu, the natural name, not man-made, the only name of the Nameless, which all nature constantly proclaims."

—Hazrat Khan
*The Sufi Message of Hazrat
Inayat Khan, Book 2*[1]

Each being is constantly telling its story and singing its own unique song. When our spiritual ears are open, we will hear each tree whispering its history, purpose, and love for us. A forest will enchant us with its symphony of sound comprised of every tree, shrub, and flower within its boundary. Artists and musicians will abandon the cities and flock to the musical forest. Poets will gather in the clearings and write inspirational words when they are attuned to this music of creation sometimes called "the Music of the Spheres."

However, few notice this symphony amid the hustle and bustle of life. Even fewer hear the call of Soul to follow the Sound Current of HU back to Its source, which is the purest of love.

The Symphony of HU

Every living being in existence is constantly proclaiming its identity, adding its keynote to the song of creation. Each group of minerals, each family of plants, each species of animals, together with the human family, all add their keynotes to the chorus of the planet. Planets harmonize with other planets and then synchronize with galaxies. Even the individual planes can be identified by specific sounds.

Beginning with the physical world, these sounds include "thunder, roar of the surf, tinkle of bells, running water, and buzzing of bees." In the higher realms beyond duality, these sounds become even more enchanting: "single note of flute, heavy wind, deep humming, thousand violins, music of woodwinds, sound of a whirlpool, music of the universe, and the music of God."[2]

During one deep contemplation, I heard the sound of what must have been a thousand bagpipes. That is the closest description I can give; words cannot do it justice. The sound carried undercurrents of joy, freedom, peace, love, adventure, and more. It was as if each note contained these qualities and was expressing itself through sound.

The "song of HU" touches everything in existence with Its love. When we sing this sacred word, whether we are aware of it or not, we are communicating on the deepest level with the all-pervading consciousness of the Creator. Everything in existence came into being through this divine Light and Sound and is presently sustained by It. Sound came first; the Living Word was the original sound.

The Living Word in Motion

The universe is connected at the subatomic level by thin golden strands of light, not only in this world but in every dimension including those realms some call heaven. This underlying fabric of creation is sometimes called "the Golden Thread of Life." It is spun with love on the loom of the Creator.

Through all that lives there runs a current, flowing in a ceaseless cycle. This is the Living Word in motion. Some call It "the Spirit of HU," "Divine Spirit," or simply "Spirit." As the Living Word vibrates throughout creation, It travels upon the Golden Thread singing Its song, the song of *HU*. While It is divine love, It is also total consciousness.

Being one with Divine Spirit, the Inner Teacher can appear to us inwardly in any form with which we are comfortable. We extend the mold with our thoughts and intentions, Divine Spirit fills it, then responds to our questions and desires to the degree we can hold Its love and accept Its wisdom. The highest consciousness of the Creator will also appear to us inwardly during contemplation in various forms of Light and Sound, often as a blue light or blue star.

Divine Spirit, this current of Light and Sound, flows downward and outward from the Creator in the highest worlds. When it reaches the outermost bounds of creation, It returns. The returning wave leads home. By singing *HU*, we can tune in to the Sound Current and experience firsthand the protection, guidance, and love of the Creator.

*   *   *

Life is full of firsts: our first bicycle, our first scraped knee, our first day of school, our first love, our first broken heart, our first car, our first paycheck, etc. I'm sure you can think of several other firsts. Right up there with my first car, which was a '66 Mustang, by the way, is the first time I heard the mysterious "sound of silence" at the age of five.

The Sound of Falling Snow

Little did I know that I had arrived at a crossroads that chilly morning when I stopped to listen to the sound of falling snow. Had I not paused to catch my breath after climbing a small knoll, and had it not been so incredibly quiet in the remote location where my family lived, I might never have heard it. I stopped to appreciate the huge snowflakes that had been falling for most of the morning. The boughs of the evergreen trees were even more beautiful than when they wore only green. It was a picture postcard scene.

I could see our house in the distance, the one provided by the mining company where my father was employed as superintendent. Lazy plumes of smoke drifted heavenward from our chimney. I'd been given permission to roam the surrounding hills in search of a Christmas tree that my father would chop down later. Maybe I would find a bicycle under the tree this year!

Then, all thoughts about presents suddenly vanished as I stood motionless, absorbing the scene before me. I could hear my own heart beating. Mesmerized, I gazed out across the valley, now clad in a garment of white. The snowflakes seemed to be making a very delicate, barely audible sound as they landed. *But was I hearing the sound of falling snow or something else?* I wondered. It was an ever so gentle "shush, shush" sound. My intuition told me this unknown sound was coming from behind the snowflakes. I sensed that I was experiencing something special, possibly even divine.

"Someday I will discover what that sound is," I told myself. It was roughly sixteen years later that I was loaned a copy of *The Tiger's Fang*, by Paul Twitchell, and learned about the Sound Current of HU. The sound I had heard behind the curtain of snowflakes was one of Its myriad expressions. That day, long ago, I heard the sound behind all sounds and recognized it as something significant. I had no idea how important of a role it would play in my life.

*   *   *

Oi remembers a spiritual first which occurred when she was in her early twenties living in Bangkok, Thailand. She was a practicing Buddhist at the time.

A Gift in a Golden Box

Over ninety percent of the Thai population are Buddhists, and I consider myself fortunate to have found the teachings of Eckankar[3] in this lifetime. When I first read the word "ECKANKAR" in gold letters on a light blue flyer in 1994, I felt an immediate connection. *Had I been a student of these teachings in my previous life?* I wondered.

In 1995, I had a vivid dream the night before my first Eckankar seminar in Bangkok. I was walking on a peaceful shore under a starry night sky. The rhythmic lapping of the waves soothed me. I could feel a warm, gentle breeze kissing my face and soft sand caressing my feet. Directly in front of me, there was a man holding a shimmering golden box in his hands. As I approached him, he greeted me with a welcoming smile and extended his arms. "This is for you," he announced.

I accepted the gift wholeheartedly. When I opened the box, a brilliant blue light emerged. It illuminated my surroundings and touched the stars. Reflecting on the dream, I wondered if I would meet this mysterious man again and learn more about the magnificent blue light.

The next morning, I awoke with a feeling of great anticipation. When I arrived at the seminar, I was surprised to find myself the only Thai person among the group of approximately twelve attendees. The rest were Canadians, East Indians, Malaysians, and some Americans.

In our group discussion, I noticed an individual from Malaysia sitting next to me. He looked familiar. For some reason, I felt a strong kinship with him as if he were an old friend. I suddenly realized that he was the person I had met in my dream the night before. During one of our breaks, I followed my intuition and shared my inner experience, then asked if he knew the significance of the beautiful blue light.

The Malaysian man listened with interest and kindly replied, "The blue light is a form of the Mahanta, the Inner Teacher. I was serving as a vehicle for this great being to give you the gift of his love. He is always with you, whether in human form or the blue light of Spirit."

I thanked the man for his wonderful insight. Feeling elated, I left the seminar knowing that my life would never be the same.

*   *   *

One purpose for writing this book is to introduce the Sanctuary of HU. A second purpose, according to the Inner Teacher, is to write about the reality of HU and the benefits of singing the sacred word. As I picked up my pen, a strong nudge came through to include a few words about those subtle inner experiences, the ones that can easily be passed off as imagination.

Deciding whether or not they are real can be one of the most difficult and perplexing challenges we face as spiritual students, even with the guidance of Spirit. I have been aware of words playing in the background of my consciousness before, for instance, and simply ignored them, passing them off as inconsequential. Thankfully, this time, as I was driving home from the river, I recognized their importance.

Had Divine Spirit not arranged this memorable inner experience, this book would not have been written. I am also aware that, somewhere along the way, I must have earned a certain degree of trust from the Inner Teacher.

One such case occurred shortly after returning from a sojourn in Mexico while in my mid-thirties. Looking back, I can now see how this encounter with a powerful spiritual adept served to open the door these many years later for our current project. Had I not trusted my inner senses back then, it is possible that Oi and I would not have been granted this opportunity to write about the House of the Living Word and The Golden Book of HU.

A Question of Trust

While driving alone on a busy street late one morning, my mind began to race when I thought I heard someone ask a question. It was not a physical voice, but a subtle, inner impression. It had come out of the blue: "Would you like to go further?"

Despite the uncertainty that I had even heard someone ask the question, I answered offhandedly, "Yes, I'd like to go further."

"Very well," came the response. "If you're serious, then meet me at the bench near the waterfall by nightfall." The words were accompanied by a short, abrupt nod.

What did it mean to go further? I wondered. Had I heard correctly, or was this whole conversation simply my imagination? I wasn't totally sure. To be safe, I resolved to leave town immediately and make the one-hour drive to a popular hiking destination north of Glide, Oregon. Another half hour's trek from the parking lot would get me to the bench near the waterfall well before dusk. The one-mile, round trip to the falls was one of my favorites. Even if I had imagined the whole conversation, some fresh air would do me good, I reasoned.

Just then, the secretary at my brother's real estate office called to say that I was needed across town right away to meet with a potential renter—not what I wanted to hear. I'd have to skip lunch. And then two more time-consuming emergencies came up. It was getting late. There was still time to make the drive, but I was becoming nervous. The traffic was heavier than usual, even though rush hour had been over for nearly forty-five minutes. I glanced down at my gas gauge. It was almost on empty.

By the time I finally pulled into the parking lot at the base of the trail leading to the waterfall, the sun was setting. I reached for my flashlight, the one I always kept with me in the glove compartment. To my dismay, it was gone. Common sense and a healthy dose of skepticism told me to go back home; however, curiosity and determination urged me forward. At worst, I thought to myself, I'd get lost in the darkness and have to spend the night on the trail. But there was also the possibility that something life changing might happen. So, I stumbled onward through the last light of day toward a potential meeting with destiny.

A deer jumped out from a thicket beside me, scattering loose rock with its hooves as it bounded up the trail ahead. My heart began to pound heavily. How different the woods appear at night. In the dying light of day, I could just make out the bench about twenty yards away. No one was there.

I was relieved, but I was also a little disappointed. As a symbolic gesture, I bent down and touched the arm of the bench with a forefinger. I wheeled about without stopping to rest, wondering how I would make it safely to the bottom with a new moon as my only guide.

As I felt my way down the trail, I heard the words of the unseen Adept reverberating through my consciousness. "Very well," he said matter-of-factly, "the easy part's over."

The easy part's over? I repeated the words slowly, trying to understand what I had heard: The easy part's over. Not a pleasant thought considering what I'd gone through already. I won't go into detail, but the list was substantial.

I heaved a sigh of relief when I finally found my way to the parking lot in the inky blackness—so far, so good. As I turned onto the highway, my mind reached out toward an uncertain future.

"How bad could it be?" I asked myself with a nervous laugh. "I've lost everything in my life at one point or another except my sense of humor." But alas, a time would come when I'd lose that, too. Thankfully, it would be only temporary.

Another one of those questionable inner experiences centered around writing this book. Although I have grown more confident in my ability to recognize subtle messages over the years, invariably, there came a day when I found myself doubting my conversations with the Voice of HU. I wondered, *Why haven't I ever heard of It before? Is my imagination simply coloring outside the lines?* A waking dream message put my mind at ease.

A Cosmic Sea of Words

Oi and I originally estimated that we'd complete the first draft of this book sometime late in 2022. She had her own project, and I had outlines for two other books vying for attention. But after words began flowing about the existence of The Golden Book of HU, I became excited. For two solid months, it was all I thought about. At the end of that period, I had written several thousand words. Oi could catch up later.

While my computer graphic skills are limited by my Mac Pages program, I threw myself into designing some covers. Oi and I had recently worked with Claude Gruffy, a world-class Canadian artist.[4] Prior to sending him a copy of my original front and back draft covers, I shared them with Oi.

The wording on the back revealed details of which she was currently unaware. It was the first time Oi had heard the term, "the Voice of HU," or the location of Param Akshar. I told myself I didn't want to burden her with details associated with writing another book while she was finishing a book of her own, but, truthfully, the real reason was that I harbored doubts about the authenticity of my experiences. After reading the back cover wording over my shoulder on the computer screen, Oi gave me a questioning look.

She asked if the Temple of Param Akshar was really on the Soul Plane. I assumed that it was, but I had no way of knowing other than my trust in the Voice of HU. I vaguely recalled hearing or reading about the temple when I was in my twenties.

Oi sorted through the various books in our bookcase and produced one called *A Cosmic Sea of Words: The ECKANKAR Lexicon*.[5] It was one of the many I had not yet read. I held my breath as she opened it. To my surprise, delight, and relief, the temple was listed and described as follows:

Param Akshar. *PAH-rahm AHK-shar*
The Temple of Golden Wisdom, the House of Imperishable Knowledge, on the Soul Plane, the Atma Lok; Supreme Lord; another name for God.[6]

Oi then flipped through the *Lexicon* saying, "Let's see if it has the Voice of HU."

"Oh, that won't be in there," I responded with a chuckle.

Oi's eyes lit up. "It's here!" she exclaimed.

I felt ripples of excitement running through my body as I waited for her to read the definition:

Voice of HU.

The Spirit; often known as the Sugmad, the true name of God in the upper realms. See also Law of HU; Principle of HU; Universal Spirit of HU.[7]

I was noticeably relieved when Oi and I finished our Conversations with Honey session that morning. I felt almost giddy, as she returned *A Cosmic Sea of Words* to its place in our bookcase.

While I have learned to trust my silent conversations with the Inner Teacher, I found it interesting that the Voice of HU felt it necessary to verify some of the information I had received during the early stages of writing. After this confirmation, I approached my daily contemplations with even more diligence. Suffice it to say, I had a greater respect for the project and felt a little more weight on my shoulders to report accurately on both The Golden Book and the Voice of HU.

- 3 -
Dreams and the Dream Teacher

*"Your vision will become clear
only when you can look into your own heart.
Who looks outside, dreams; who looks inside, awakes."*

—Carl Jung[1]

A waking dream informed me that something was missing. Since this book was our primary point of focus, I took this to mean that something was missing from the chapter we were working on—this one.

Everything in my life needs to be in its proper place; messy is okay, as long as it's in its place. When I noticed that a ring holding up the shower curtain was missing, I looked everywhere. Finally, I asked Oi about it. She had noticed it on the floor, assumed it was broken because it was twisted, and threw it away. These particular shower curtain hangers snap together from their open, twisted position. Later, I found it in the garbage, reattached it, and breathed a sigh of satisfaction.

Oi and I talked about this waking dream of "something missing." She asked me if I had considered writing about dreams or the Dream Teacher. Intuitively, I knew that Oi was being a channel for Divine Spirit.

The Inner Teacher guides, instructs, and protects those under his care at night in the dream state, where he is known as the Dream Teacher. He may appear in guises familiar to the dreamer or remain cloaked in pure consciousness. He will not work with the dreamer unless invited to do so.

When asked, he can show us our past to help us better understand our current circumstances regarding health, relationships, career, and other relevant aspects of our life. Balancing karma is often accomplished in the dream state where it is more convenient and less stressful. The Dream Teacher, through Soul Travel, can help us overcome the fear of death. He can escort us to places in the spiritual worlds—Temples of Golden Wisdom—where adepts teach students dedicated to finding truth.

The secret teachings of the ages are generally first introduced through our dreams. I first became aware of the Dream Teacher's handiwork when I was fourteen. The dream which follows seemed unusual at the time considering my Christian upbringing.

"Now Playing: The Song of HU"
At the conclusion of my eighth-grade year, I had a curious dream which stood out for a couple of reasons. One, I remembered so few of my dreams; and two, the unexplainable attraction I felt for what I called "that word." The dream was set in Eugene, home of the University of Oregon, an hour north of my hometown on I–5.

While walking near the college in my dream, I found the area somewhat familiar: coffee shops, clothing stores, and a bookstore situated next to a pizza parlor where students were socializing. My friend, Ted, bounded ahead. He crossed a busy street and called back for me to follow. I had stopped to survey an old building across from the bookstore.

It appeared to have been vacant for a very long time. I could see cobwebs on the inside of its semi-darkened windows, dust thickly caked on the outside walls, and an entry that was empty save for wind-blown leaves. Ted followed my gaze to see what I had found so captivating. Honestly, I didn't know. I stood transfixed, staring up at the marquee of what I realized was an abandoned theater.

The name of the latest movie was displayed in large white letters upon the dark blue background of the theater's marquee. I felt a tingling sensation as I read it aloud: "Now Playing: The Song of HU." I awoke with the name on my lips, wondering what the movie was all about.

The answer came seven years later when a high school classmate pulled up in front of my house in his faded red Volkswagen. Dave had returned from the service and stopped by to say hello. A short article about out-of-the-body travel was taped to his back, passenger-side window. It explained how one could leave the physical body and visit temples of esoteric learning beyond this realm.

I read about a wave of spiritual energy—pure love—that flowed out of the heart of God. By singing the word *"HU,"* it was possible to connect with the returning wave of the song of HU and ride with It back to the Source.

Soon thereafter, I began reading books about the out-of-the-body state written by Paul Twitchell and others. I shared these books with Ted, but he passed on the opportunity to learn more about the song of HU just as he'd continued down the sidewalk in my dream. It seems old movies just aren't for everyone.

The Black Jaguar

Recently, I reminisced about the many joyful hours I had spent on the softball field with my brother and a loosely knit circle of friends. Throughout my twenties, slow-pitch softball provided quality entertainment and a variety of interesting social opportunities. During this time, the Inner Teacher threw in some valuable lessons centering mostly around common sense, good judgment, and self-control.

These tests often took place at the local pizza parlor after each game where our sponsor generously purchased pitcher after pitcher of beer in celebration of a win or to drown our sorrows after swallowing a tough defeat. One evening, after a rather spectacular victory, the beer was flowing in amounts commensurate to the exuberance the team was feeling. When someone filled the glass of our catcher seated across from me, the frothy beer overflowed its mug. As I watched it dripping upon the table, I remembered an unsettling dream from a few nights before.

I found myself staring into the eyes of a jaguar. He was sleek and black with a sapphire-blue collar wrapped around his neck. He was my friend. Playfully, we chased each other around the boxing ring we occupied. When we grew tired, the jaguar would lay his head upon the upper rope and purr contentedly as I stroked its head.

But when it came time for me to go, a dramatic change came over the animal. As I made my way across the canvas, I heard a faint growl from behind. It became louder and more threatening as I attempted to leave. To my surprise, when I turned around, the beautiful jaguar had transformed into a different creature altogether. His once sleek fur was now dull orange. Patches of fur had fallen out due to some disease. Fur stood on end at the back of its neck. The jaguar's clear blue eyes were now blood red. Saliva foamed from its exposed fangs and dripped upon the canvas below.

Whenever I stopped, the jaguar would relax. But each time I made the slightest attempt to go, it would growl more menacingly. To leave the ring would be dangerous, for the jaguar intended to hold me in its power forever. I awoke in a cold sweat and puzzled over the meaning of the vivid dream most of the following day.

Watching the foam dripping from the frosty glass of beer, I understood. Alcohol had been my friend for many years, but now our relationship had changed. As time had passed, alcohol demanded more and more of my attention. The Dream Teacher was showing me that the black jaguar was not my friend; it was my captor.

Throughout that summer, I fought to free myself from the grip of alcohol. While I lost many battles, I finally won the war. Without the Inner Teacher's guidance and support, this would not have been possible. I filed this victory away under the category of "Lesson Learned in Self Control."

My teammates tolerated my behavioral change, perhaps because I was an integral part of the team; however, to them, it didn't make sense to pass up free beer. The only one celebrating with me was the Dream Teacher.

With the exception of a few powerful dreams like this one, my guidance from the Divine stems mostly from waking dreams. But, in one instance, the Dream Teacher utilized both dreams and waking dreams in tandem to shed light on my past and instill confidence in my newfound interest in writing.

The Flying Book

Growing up, while others were happily discussing their nightly dreams and offering meaningful interpretations, I would sit silently in the corner. I suspected that my dream life had been blackballed from joining the "Dream Weavers Country Club." But I soldiered on, making adjustments along the way.

A major breakthrough came when I began noticing symbolic messages hidden in plain sight in my day-to-day life. Even in grade school, I would notice them and wonder if anyone else was having such strange revelations. Had I been able to reap the benefits of dreams like so many of my friends, perhaps I would not have put so much attention on waking dreams. I was exceedingly pleased, however, when the Dream Teacher surprised me with a one-day pass to the country club of my dreams.

A lot changed in my life during the time I lived in Hawaii. I would have liked to say that I began to grow up spiritually well before the age of twenty-eight, but it just isn't so. I'd tasted success, including my triumph over alcohol, but up until my close call in the Waikiki surf, I took life for granted and spent most of my time daydreaming and chasing the sun.

When I began having a peculiar recurring dream about digging a square pit in a remote wooded area next to a body of water, I passed it off as more "dream nonsense." But I had to admit, I was giving those dreams more attention than usual, perhaps because I was unemployed at the time and had nothing better to do while tanning on Waikiki Beach. I even went so far as to peruse the section on dreams in the Honolulu Public Library.

The ground was hard in my dream. I hit thick tree roots, which made the digging slow and laborious. *What could this possibly mean?* I wondered. *What connection did digging a square hole have with my beach bum life in Hawaii?*

Despite my irritation, I did something right: I asked a question. And by doing so, the Inner Teacher was able to step in with an answer. A bookstore was located near my rented condominium. One day, while browsing down an aisle containing a small section of biographies, an anthology of early American writers literally flew off the shelf and through my open arms. Startled, I picked the book up from the floor, opened it, and began reading a random passage.

The paragraph described the author's misfortune while digging a root cellar for his cabin. He had hit thick tree roots, making the excavation slow and tedious. My eyes opened wide. I turned to an essay in the book written by the same author. What little writing I had done in this life was surprisingly similar to the rhythm of the words I was reading. Sadly, this author had died believing himself to be a failure.

While I didn't know for certain whether or not I was being shown something from my own past, I did feel a wave of confidence sweep through me. Perhaps I could write a book someday, myself. This incident fit the description of a waking dream. I felt the universe smiling with me that day as I walked out of the bookstore. I was thankful that I'd finally been shown a connection between my inner world of dreams and my outer life. The Inner Teacher utilized a similar dream/waking dream scenario when Oi requested guidance about a family relationship.

Write it Down by Pichaya

There are 131 spiritual exercises listed in the book, *The Spiritual Exercises of ECK*, by Harold Klemp. In 2010, I began focusing on one called "Write It Down" in order to understand my present life and heal from my past.[2] The Dream Teacher offered insights through a series of powerful dreams.

As a way of healing, I was instructed to write down all of my challenges. Unfortunately, I had carried many of them since childhood when I had been subjected to hurtful and demeaning remarks about my appearance and intellect. Those unkind words pierced my heart and left me feeling inadequate, shameful, and unworthy of love.

It is one thing to be judged by others outside the family and quite another when it is coming from your own father. I felt unloved by him. He looked down on me and predicted that I would never succeed at anything in life. In contrast, I was fortunate to have had an angelic grandmother and a loving mother who believed in me completely and supported me in every way possible.

My heart was filled with bitterness, resentment, and anger toward my father. I was determined to prove to him that his perception of me was inaccurate. Diligently, I studied Linguistics and Mass Communications at Ramkhamhaeng University and, to his surprise, finished within three years with a bachelor's degree in English. Still, in his eyes, I was not good enough.

During the process of writing down my challenges, the Dream Teacher gave me insights through dreams about my relationship with my father. I was shown that we had been together in many lifetimes. I was the one who had been abusive then. The scenes were brutal, terrible, and cruel. I realized that I had come into this life with a karmic debt that had to be paid in the true coin.

The Dream Teacher helped me discover the root cause of my karmic relationship with my father. Through understanding the Law of Cause and Effect, I was able to take full responsibility for the harm I had caused him in previous lifetimes. Then, I was able to let go of my anger, stop blaming him, and heal.

Param Akshar by Pichaya

Every day, I sing *HU* for twenty minutes and contemplate before beginning to write. I call this sacred time of communion with the Divine, "Satsang with the Inner Teacher." Ideas often flow around three o'clock. One morning, I was guided to open a specific journal to an entry from 2015.

I was surprised to find my drawing of the Temple of Golden Wisdom I had visited in my dream. For several years, I have practiced a spiritual exercise called "The Door of Soul."[3] I present a request to the Inner Teacher and repeat these words:

"I give you permission to take me into the Far Country, to the place that is right for me now."

On the night of December 1st, I found myself at the door of a temple with the Dream Teacher. The guardian of this temple greeted us in silence with a gentle smile. He had short blonde hair and beautiful blue eyes. Extending his left hand, he slowly gestured for us to enter.

The Dream Teacher escorted me inside the temple where I saw a large golden book resting upon a pedestal. The warm glow from the book illuminated the entire room. Before I could read any words, I was awakened from the dream.

The following week, a friend and I had a discussion in her home about the Temples of Golden Wisdom. I asked if she had met any of the adepts overseeing the temples. She pointed to a picture in a frame on her dresser. Surprisingly, it was a picture of the adept I had seen in my dream. My friend told me that his name was Nirguna Ekam, the adept in charge of the Temple of Param Akshar on the Soul Plane.

One may meet the spiritual teachers responsible for each temple by chanting their names. For example, if we would like to meet Nirguna Ekam, pronounced "neer-GOO-nah EHK-ahm,"[4] at Param Akshar in the dream state, we can chant his name before going to sleep. Similarly, we can sing the word "Gopal" in two syllables with the accent on the first (GOH-pal).[5] Gopal Das oversees the Temple of Askleposis on the Astral Plane. The guardians of other Temples of Golden Wisdom, and how to properly pronounce their names, can be found in *A Cosmic Sea of Words: The Eckankar Lexicon.*

*   *   *

Oi's story reveals how the Inner Teacher loves, guides, and protects those under his care in the dream state. Occasionally, the Dream Teacher will give us glimpses into the splendors which await us in the worlds of pure Spirit. As I learned in my late twenties, now back in Oregon, he holds the keys that unlock every door.

The Universal Song of HU

Why had I been selected to receive such a rare and meritorious gift? I wondered. *Was it because of my strict dedication to the spiritual disciplines?* I smiled. Not likely. *Was it because many years hence I'd be writing about the universality of HU?* Perhaps.

Life had been kind to me since returning from Hawaii: walks in the woods, softball on weekends, and socializing with friends. Occasional naps were an added luxury. But when I drifted into the twilight area between sleep and waking consciousness late one afternoon, I felt lost, lonely, and afraid.

I had closed my eyes for only a moment when I found myself in a vast, dark cavern system. *Am I dreaming?* I wondered. The emotions felt so real. A narrow pathway led upward, hugging one wall, to an unknown destination. I kept moving higher. The oppressive environment below had become intolerable. The path emptied into a huge open area which reminded me of the receiving hall of a large indoor arena. Only, this time, I was not entering the facility to enjoy a game, I was escaping from the depths of a dark subterranean world.

My heart was beating rapidly as I rushed for the bank of doors leading outside to freedom. Suddenly, detecting movement, several malevolent beings appeared before me. No Soul was allowed to break free when they were on duty.

Nearing the doors, I could see sunlight streaming in through the windows above. I pushed down on a door handle and threw all my weight against the solid metal door. My heart sank—it was locked.

To my astonishment, a luminous being emerged from the shadows, to my left. As he approached, the guards stepped back and looked away. The Inner Teacher's hand pushed gently on the door handle next to mine. It opened easily.

"Allow me," he said graciously, holding the door open for me to pass.

Feelings of absolute relief swept through my body as I breathed in an essence of which I had never known—freedom. I thanked the Inner Teacher profusely, who was immediately recognized and greeted with respect by a crowd that had gathered around us. They had come from an outdoor stadium nearby, one concealed beyond an elevated rim.

When my eyes had adjusted, I received a shock. These beings were nothing more than globes of light, approximately six feet in diameter. Yet, each one was different with distinct facial features comparable to those on earth. Horizontal bands of color, perhaps twelve in number, danced and shimmered when they spoke. I could understand their words as impressions within my consciousness. When I turned my attention to my own body, I was surprised to discover that my form mirrored theirs—a perfect sphere of light.

As I looked around, my senses were inundated with millions of colors. There were flowers of every shade and variety imaginable, including islands of iridescent roses. The grass was carpetlike and trimmed to perfection. Pools of living water fed streams which emptied into singing rivers. What struck me most was the feeling of tranquility permeating this resplendent world. How could I tell those languishing in the caverns below about such wonders?

The most beautiful sound I had ever heard emanated from the stadium and echoed throughout the land. It was the song of HU, sung by a multitude so vast that it exceeded my imagination. From horizon to horizon, the sweet sound of HU filled the peaceful atmosphere with the purest nectar of love.

A wave of joy flowing out of my heart prompted me to join in, but as I sang *HUuuu*, my voice cracked. Hearing the inharmonious tone, several beings glanced in my direction.

An individual to my immediate right responded with an understanding smile, "You must have been away for a very long time."

"Yes," I answered quietly, holding back the tears, "a long, long time."

- 4 -
THE HIMALAYAN TEMPLE

"Spirituality cannot be taught, but caught."

—Paul Twitchell
ECKANKAR, The Key to Secret Worlds[1]

Writing about my experiences with the Dream Teacher sent me on a trip down memory lane. While outlining this chapter, I revisited my impressions of a Temple of Golden Wisdom in the Himalayas. Since I had been taken there in the Soul body by a spiritual guide, this temple could easily have been located on a supra-physical level rather than the solid material world.

My first visit to "The Himalayan Temple" was at age fourteen, just a few days after seeing "The Song of HU" in the dream state. Much later, I recognized my guide as Peddar Zaskq, the spiritual name of Paul Twitchell, a renowned spiritual teacher. He introduced me to the Abbot of the monastery on that first trip. The Himalayan Temple reminds me of a rustic lodge clinging tenaciously to the side of an extremely steep mountain. The mountain and the secluded valley below are covered with snow a good portion of the year.

I am vaguely familiar with another Temple of Golden Wisdom in Tibet, as I was also escorted there by Peddar

Zaskq. One generally has to ask to be taken to such temples to study before falling asleep at night. This second temple sits in the middle of what feels like a medieval village, hidden away from the rest of the world. Another spiritual teacher of the highest order is in charge of this temple where students come to learn in the dream state.

Then, on my trip down memory lane, I remembered the kindness of a female spiritual teacher named Kata Daki,[2] who has been in my life since I was young. Kata works with the downtrodden, hopeless, and the gravely ill. Twice in my life, she has come to my rescue when I faced serious crises.

At the age of twenty-three, I was struggling with a heavy load of karma. I was impatient. Blame it on the impetuousness of youth. I asked the Inner Teacher to speed things up when it came to resolving my karma. The load was way too much, and I crossed the line from sanity into a dark abyss. Suicide seemed like the only way out to my dazed and confused mind.

One night, Kata appeared in a dream at the bottom of a flight of stairs. She was wearing a flowing blue gown that shimmered in the moonlight. Kata told me I had two important missions ahead in life. One involved writing; the other was from a higher plane, she said, without revealing specifics. Upon apologizing to my Teacher for my impatience the following morning, my consciousness immediately brightened. My life had completely returned to normal by dinner time.

The adept at the bench near the waterfall was spot on about the easy part being over. A few years after that rendezvous, I again contemplated suicide. Once again, it was Kata Daki who came to my rescue.

I could feel Kata's presence with me the day I collapsed from a toxic overload of heavy metals and chemicals I had taken in while working at a plywood mill in my twenties.

During an aggressive cleanse, the chemicals were released with mercury thrown in for good measure. They immediately overwhelmed my body, breaking through the blood-brain barrier. Had Kata not showered me with love and support throughout the night and in the weeks that followed, without a doubt, I wouldn't be alive today.

Each spiritual teacher has his or her own strengths and unique personality, but they all have at least two things in common: they have all dedicated their lives to serving others, and they all love HU.

*   *   *

For the diet I'm currently following, I've turned to almond milk as an alternative to dairy. Oi has learned to make our own which is richer than the watered down version found in stores. She saves the pulp for energy balls and dairy-free cream cheese; the peels make good compost.

In similar fashion, the Inner Teacher utilizes all of our experiences at the appropriate time. This is how a personal story from many years back about The Himalayan Temple found its way into this book.

Following an inner nudge, I decided to move most of what I had originally written in this chapter to Chapter Twelve. This left me with a dilemma—what to include in the remainder of this one, a key position in the book?

In a contemplation, I met the Inner Teacher in his office at Param Akshar for a consultation and asked for direction. (More about my impressions of this Soul Plane office in Chapter Five.) In his kind, unassuming way, he suggested, "Why don't you write about The Himalayan Temple?"

Was the Teacher giving me the green light to reveal what I had witnessed in the room where an ancient "Book of Wisdom" is kept? I wasn't sure. But this was the image that flashed across my inner screen.

"I suppose I could write about my experience in 'the book room' without giving away any sensitive details," I said introspectively.

The Teacher nodded in agreement. "Sure," he answered quietly. I detected an unspoken tone of caution in his reply.

* * *

One may visit these Temples of Golden Wisdom in the Soul body in the company of the Inner Teacher. Often we are not aware of his presence, but he is always with us in consciousness, as close as our heartbeat.

Traveling in the Soul body is as simple as shifting our attention. Unlike physical transportation, there are no bags to pack or maps to study. Parking at airports is never a problem. But there are places in the spiritual worlds, such as Temples of Golden Wisdom, that are off-limits unless accompanied by a qualified spiritual teacher.

In the Book Room

I was not aware of the Inner Teacher's presence with me in the book room at The Himalayan Temple, but I am certain he was there in Spirit. I let my attention wander during an afternoon contemplation and suddenly became aware of a book sitting on a stand near the center of a dimly lit room. I'd seen the Book of Wisdom at least one other time during my contemplations.

I noticed a light radiating in all directions from the pages of the open book. It was roughly the shape of a flame which rose to a height of about three feet. Approaching the book, I happened to notice a glint of light reflecting brightly off the surface of an object positioned several feet behind the stand. It appeared to be metallic in nature. Just then, I noticed a swirling energy powering up in the room from out of the ethers. This was noticeable, tangible, real....

As I was preparing to write about the audible portion of this experience, I received a warning. It came in the form of a waking dream. Apparently, to give additional details would violate the Law of Silence. Rarely did I get such warnings; therefore, I took it very seriously.

The Warning

Oi and I climbed into our "seasoned" BMW on April 9th, 2022, on our way to a memorial service for Mike, the star basketball player on my high school team. To my dismay, I discovered that the computerized information screen in the center of the dashboard had gone dark. Furthermore, the passenger side mirror needed manual adjusting since going through the car wash in advance of our two-hour trip south.

My heart sank as I stared down at a warning icon above the speedometer. It was the outline of a sword with "SOS" printed across it. Oi looked up the meaning of the symbol on the Internet. It indicated a problem with the "audible" portion of the information screen. A second warning light alerted us that the driver's side headlight was also out.

The meaning of this powerful waking dream message was clear to me: *Don't write about the audible portion of the experience in the book room.* I interpreted the driver's-side headlight warning as further guidance to keep my personal revelations to myself as well.

As we neared the site where the memorial was being held, I voiced out loud to the Inner Teacher, "Okay, message received. Can you please return the car to normal now?"

Two hours later, we left Mike's memorial and headed home. Excitedly, Oi pointed to the information center of our car. It was now lit up and working perfectly.

I discovered that a new headlight for our BMW would cost over $2,000 with installation. Divine Spirit had my attention. If nearly violating the Law of Silence came with such a hefty price tag, it was clear that I needed to take steps to ensure that I didn't actually cross that line. I contemplated on appropriate waking dream symbols which could tell me when I would need to pause and review what I was about to write or say.

"Bookmark" waking dreams can tell us when an opportune time has arrived to sell our present home, look for a better job, begin a new relationship, etc. They can also warn us when we're about to violate any of the spiritual laws. The image I selected to represent the Law of Silence was a garment turned inside out such as a T-shirt. This would indicate that something on the inside should not be exposed to the outside world. A broken red pen lying on the ground would also represent the same message: "Keep silent."

Oi and I always choose symbols which do no harm. For example, using a lost dog or a dead animal for a Bookmark could result in some unfortunate events and karmic debts. We also choose symbols that don't regularly appear in our lives but can easily be manifested by Spirt whenever appropriate. My two "all clear" signs are "three of the same number aligned in a row" (333, 777, 999, etc.) and "a bird perched on the very top of a tree or pole."

Ripples on the Pond

I remembered an insight that a friend had been given by a spiritual teacher. He was advised: "When you walk upon the water, leave no ripples on the pond."

Is writing about the Sanctuary and the Golden Book of HU a violation of the Law of Silence? I wondered. If so, I decided that I would abandon the project in this early stage. My stomach was churning. How could I break this news to Oi? Then, I felt the Inner Teacher's comforting presence as he responded to my urgent concern:

"Ripples have their place, you know. As a writer and teacher, how can you not leave ripples? But there is a time for everything. The trick is knowing when to sit quietly on the shore and when to dive into the water to help another Soul, even if swimming is not allowed.

"In many instances, such as initiations, spiritual tests, and confidential conversations, the Law of Silence must be honored. Waking dreams can clearly tell you when it is prudent to keep quiet—as you recently discovered with your car. The information from the Voice of HU will, potentially, help many Souls better understand how magnificent they truly are as spiritual beings.

"When revealing sensitive details is necessary to the overall story, ask yourself, are your words written to entertain and teach or to bolster the ego? Also, ask if the information is harmful or uplifting. Will it impede the progress of other Souls or inspire them to continue onward as their energies wane? When in doubt, ask, and I will answer. You were given the freedom to write a book that you'd enjoy reading. This still holds true, but it is important to temper enthusiasm with a healthy measure of discernment."

I thanked the Inner Teacher for his reassuring words. His answer regarding the Law of Silence left me feeling a little more at ease. With these guidelines in mind, I revisited everything I had written very carefully and found another cause for concern. While I was now comfortable sharing some of the information from the Voice of HU, I realized that certain portions would push the envelope of believability.

Another waking dream provided guidance about this. On our way to the market, Oi and I stopped at a traffic light behind a delivery truck. We were discussing how much information we could comfortably share. A sign posted on the rear cargo area of the truck read: LIMIT 65. I was being advised that we could explore metaphorically any side road that called to us, but our authority to release new ideas and information had a limit. I set up another Bookmark waking dream which would indicate when we had reached or exceeded that limit.

I chose a large black and gray feather as this symbol. At its appearance, I would go back and examine what I had recently written. Amazingly, only three hours after choosing the Bookmark, I found a feather on the ground at a nearby pond matching this exact description. It would be necessary to make a quick U-turn and revisit what I had written thus far in the book. I utilized the same all clear signs that I had selected for the Law of Silence—three of the same number in a row and a bird on the very top of a tree or pole. However, I added a third: finding a small white feather in an unusual circumstance.

*   *   *

When I checked the word count again for this chapter, I found that half of the pages were still yet to be filled. This is seldom the case for me. *How would I complete it?* An old football adage came to mind: "When in doubt, punt." My version of punting is to defer to the Inner Teacher. *Why not punt? After all, he is the architect of the project. I'm just the guy carrying the lunch pail and hammer to work.*

I poured a steaming cup of tea, telling myself that inspiration would now flow. While the dam didn't break, I did get a subtle message from the Inner Teacher to stay on course with The Himalayan Temple theme.

"Be ready for something new," I was told.

Impressions of the Abbot

"Something new" was a meeting with the Abbot of the Temple, Fubbi Quantz. The Inner Teacher had arranged it. I had met Fubbi before in this lifetime, but the memories were vague. My impression of him stemmed mostly from a drawing I'd seen displayed on a website.[3] I pictured him as a somewhat rigid, straightforward, serious kind of instructor.

While his responsibilities demand that he pay close attention to monastery business, I found him to be extremely cordial, even friendly toward me. I could tell the Abbot loved his job and those Souls with whom he worked closely within the monastery.

On my first trip to this temple with Peddar Zaskq in 1966, I had no idea who he was or where we were going. I remember touching down on a mountain ridge leading to a building. After crossing a wooden walkway, perhaps twenty feet in width, we entered a long receiving hall and were greeted by a rather tall man wearing a floor-length white robe with a hood pulled up over his head. He was standing in front of two wooden doors at the end of the hall.

Peddar spoke briefly to this man in a quiet tone and then tilted his head sideways toward me. "He is here to learn," he said, then wheeled about and left abruptly. As the tall man in the hooded white robe held the door open for me to enter, I remember thinking to myself, *How am I ever go-*

ing to get home? Is this man who brought me here—someone I've never met—just going to leave me here? But I felt safe with this stranger, whom I later learned was the Abbot of this Temple of Golden Wisdom.

Somehow, I did get home because I awoke in my bed the next morning without remembering anything after stepping inside the building with the Abbot. I did not even recall seeing the Wheel of Life painting which reportedly graces the monastery's domed ceiling.

"Do You Remember?"

Now, nearly a lifetime later, I found myself standing before the same double doors of the monastery in the presence of the Abbot. Fubbi greeted me warmly, thanking me for serving the world through writing.

If you can imagine the feeling you'd get when you walked into the Sistine Chapel for the first time and saw Michelangelo's painting, you'd come close to knowing what I experienced when I stood beside the Abbot gazing up at the ceiling. While I had likely viewed the Wheel of Life during my previous visit, this time I was able to consciously retain the memory.

The Abbot was silent. There really are no words he could have said that would have enhanced the moment. After several minutes, he spoke quietly. Fubbi asked a question of me with profound implications:

"Do you remember?"

I saw an image in my mind, a vision, which fully clarified the Abbot's question. I was standing beside him wearing a floor-length brown robe gazing up at a freshly painted section of the ceiling. I knew deep down inside that I had a past connection with the images I now stood admiring. I could have been the one tasked with cleaning up after the project, for all I know. But my heart swelled with emotions—mainly joy and satisfaction.

The Significance of Seven

Paul Twitchell wrote about the Wheel of Life in a book called *The ECK-VIDYA: Ancient Science of Prophecy,* describing the twelve nidanas, or cycles, in detail.[4] Some call it the "School of Life." These are the twelve major experiences Soul goes through as part of this cosmic curriculum.

Since reading Twitchell's book many years ago, I have often wondered why it is called the Wheel of the Eighty-four and not the Wheel of Twelve. While contemplating on the subject late one night, shortly after my interaction with the Abbot, my mind began to wander. As I was about to fall asleep, I found myself in the Soul body hovering above the small town where I had grown up.

My attention, as if guided by an invisible force, was drawn to several people in succession who had played important, yet diverse, roles in my life. There was Mr. Holley, the Police Chief, who had pulled me over more than once for speeding in my '66 Mustang while in high school. Surprisingly, he never wrote me a ticket, choosing instead to warn me about the consequences of irresponsible driving. Then, there was Mrs. Connolly, my third grade teacher who exuded kindness and was loved by her students.

My father came into focus. He was dressed in his usual tan slacks and matching tan work shirt, inspecting a sample of cinnabar, the rock from which mercury, also known as quicksilver, is extracted using extremely high heat. Although our differences were many, I appreciated his engineering and mathematical mind.

My mother appeared on my inner screen with her arms open wide in anticipation of a hug. She dabbled in arts and crafts and excelled at painting the hunting dogs my father raised and the pheasants he hunted.

In another scene, I watched Buss Conn, a heavy equipment operator, digging a trench outside the mine where my father was employed as superintendent. Buss also drove the mining train. While I was not allowed to enter the tunnel of the mine, Buss would stop the tiny train as he emerged from the darkness and invite me and my best friend, Jimmy, to ride out to the end of the track with him to dump his load of waste rock.

My attention jumped to the small church where my grandmother was a fixture. Although I squirmed and fidgeted in the hard pine pew next to her and daydreamed of playing baseball while the minister droned on about eternal damnation, I admired my grandmother's devotion to her beliefs.

And lastly, I saw in my inner vision the smiling face of Linda, a neighbor, who was self-employed as a wedding planner. She epitomized multi-tasking and was a master at organizing celebrations of every kind.

I appreciated having known all these influential people in my life. It brought me joy reuniting with them, even from afar. But I wondered, *Was there more to be learned from revisiting my past?* The quaint small-town images shifted, and I found myself in a theater observing a war movie. The seven aforementioned individuals were now playing roles in this Big Screen drama.

Mr. Holley was dressed in a military uniform bearing the insignia "MP," Military Police. Mrs. Connolly instructed new recruits on what they might expect once they deployed to a certain foreign country. My father was draped over an architectural table designing a portable pontoon bridge. My mother was writing stories, complete with colored drawings, about each of the boys in our town who had been called to service.

Buss Conn drove a tank in this movie. I watched him courageously plow his way through a muddy field in the direction of a raging battle. My grandmother, who would have been a wonderful nurse, sat alone in her favorite pew in church praying for those who had been wounded in action. And our neighbor, Linda, had joined the USO, where she was instrumental in organizing variety shows and fundraisers.

Inwardly, I heard a soft impression form into words, clarifying what I was witnessing in my inner vision.

"White light separates into seven colors of the spectrum when passed through a prism: red, blue, yellow, green, orange, violet, and indigo. These rays vibrate at specific frequencies and contain qualities that relate to seven human archetypes."

The Inner Teacher continued: *"Each of the seven people from your town, representing these archetypes, found different roles in the 'nidana of conflict,' the war movie, where their individual strengths and abilities were utilized. Their lessons and trials were also unique. Overall, rather than one experience waiting for Soul in this nidana, as you can see, there are seven. Thus, as Soul proceeds through the twelve nidanas, it plays seven different archetypal roles in each, bringing the total to eighty-four significant experiences in the School of Life."*

As the images began to fade, I fell asleep with the realization that the presence of the Inner Teacher has always been with me: in the country school listening to Mrs. Connoly read from her poetry book, riding in my first car as I sped through town in a hurry to get nowhere. He was with me shortly after graduating high school when I left my grandmother's church in disillusionment.

It is reassuring to know that, as we negotiate the challenges of the School of Life wearing different guises, we are never alone. The Inner Teacher and a host of other spiritual teachers walk with us through the darkest valleys. They rejoice with us in those golden moments we sometimes experience on our journey home to love.

COLORED RAY	ARCHETYPE
Red	Military General, policeman
Blue	Teacher, counselor
Yellow	Engineer, accountant, businessman
Green	Artist, musician, writer
Orange	Construction worker, builder
Violet	Nurse, volunteer
Indigo	Planner, organizer

Part II
Solving Life's Challenges with HU

- 5 -

THROUGH THE DOORS OF HU
AND OTHER SPIRITUAL EXERCISES

*"Live your life as if you are one with the HU,
so that every moment of your life is a spiritual exercise."*

—Harold Klemp
The Sound of Soul [1]

Once I was shown the Sanctuary of HU, my passion for writing intensified, not to mention a few fresh possibilities for spiritual exercises. Oi and I have learned that the best spiritual exercises are the ones we can't wait to practice. Examples can be found in *The Spiritual Exercises of ECK*, by Harold Klemp. Creating our own is also encouraged.

It can be frustrating when we dial the number of an Internet provider, for example, and hear a pre-recorded message listing several options, none of which includes speaking to a real person. Imagine my chagrin when I heard one of these messages playing in my mind during a contemplation. A novel thought struck me. Why not pause the recording and create a list of menu items that I'd actually like to hear? This evolved into the following spiritual exercise.

Sanctuary Switchboard

Picture in your mind a direct inner phone line connecting you to the Sanctuary of HU. Expectantly, you dial the number hoping to hear some inspiring bits of wisdom. Instead, you hear those dreaded words: "Listen closely, as our menu items have recently changed." To your surprise, the choices you're given are uplifting and helpful:

To view the Golden Book of HU, please press 1
To request a spiritual healing, please press 2
To consult with the Inner Teacher in his office, please press 3
To speak with the Voice of HU, please press 4
For a tour of the Sanctuary, please press 5
For all other matters, please press 6
If you are working on patience, please remain on the line

Over the course of several days, I selected each of the first five options. I was pleased with all of them. My experience with Option 3 was fascinating.

Routinely, I imagine meeting the Inner Teacher in his office on the Astral Plane. In my experience, it's small, unassuming, clean, and a large whiteboard sits in one corner. A half dozen chairs, which remind me of those seen in photos of kitchens from the sixties, are placed in a loose circle around the room. The Teacher is dressed casually in a light blue shirt and tan slacks. Our conversations are brief, but generally helpful. Often, he will write down key points on the board. I expected to find a similar layout in the Soul Plane facility.

This office, however, as I view it in my imagination, overlooks a placid pond where Water Lillies bloom and Swan-like birds congregate. They have striking colors, reminding me of the Mandarin Ducks Oi and I occasionally see on our walks, only much larger in size.

The Inner Teacher's Soul Plane office is but one in a greater complex. Other spiritual teachers who work closely with him also have space here and meet in a circular meeting room to discuss important business. This includes evaluating the progress of certain individuals incarnated on earth who study at the Temples of Golden Wisdom. The expertise and advice of these Adepts is sought after by Souls throughout the many dimensions both above and below the Soul Plane.

All in all, aside from a few large plants and plush carpeting, the interior of this office is a much more spacious version of the Inner Teacher's Astral Plane office. Visitors are shown great respect, and a feeling of warm camaraderie permeates the atmosphere. Many spiritual teachers make their home on the temple grounds or in the surrounding countryside as a matter of convenience, since the Soul Plane is roughly midway between the Infinite Light and the lower worlds of polarity.

On this particular visit, as the images were fading, I mused to myself, *Wouldn't Param Akshar be a great place to live one day? Was living here at the Temple what I really wanted?* It was a definite maybe.

*   *   *

The Sanctuary Doors of HU

Oi and I give credit to the Doors of HU spiritual exercise we've been listening to on the CD referenced in the Preface for inspiring us to begin this project. As soon as I began visiting the Sanctuary of HU at Param Akshar, I wondered if its doors may be the basis for the exercise mentioned in the HU song CD. We created a variation of the original exercise called *the Sanctuary doors of HU*.

Picture yourself standing with the Inner Teacher before the doors to the Sanctuary at Param Akshar. As you sing *HU*, the doors swing open revealing the magnificent Golden Book resting upon its pedestal of living gold. Let the exercise unfold. Listen for the Voice of HU or ask to be shown something of interest in the Sanctuary.

Opening The Golden Book

By asking a question and opening a book at random, an answer can be found. Allow your intuition to guide you to the appropriate book. These answers received are sometimes called "Highlighted Waking Dreams," since they often stand out as if they've been highlighted with a marking pen. The following exercise involves opening The Golden Book of HU.

Approach The Golden Book with reverence. Know that the Inner Teacher is present with you, even though you may not see him in form. Stand before the glowing Golden Book and connect with the energy field surrounding it. This is the Voice of HU, the highest aspect of the Creator. You may choose to go into the experience with a question or ask the Inner Teacher to show you what is appropriate.

Open the book near the beginning, middle, or end. You may or may not see words printed on its pages. Listen for the Voice of HU. Please be patient. Alternatively, you may be shown something later in the dream state or through a waking dream.

Discovering Your Spiritual Name

Stand in front of The Golden Book of HU and feel the love emanating from it. Ask, "Please show me my spiritual name." Listen inwardly or see your spiritual name printed on a page within the book. What details about your life as Soul follow your name? You may be surprised.

Blessings of Love and Gratitude

Blessing each meal may be viewed either as a spiritual exercise or a spiritual discipline. Oi and I see it as both. We have two people to thank for inspiring us to begin the practice of blessing our food and water—Dr. Masura Emoto, and a manager at the water district where I worked named Bob.

When Dr. Emoto published his groundbreaking books displaying photographs of water samples exposed to various words, I bought them all. Harsh words produce dark and disfigured crystals, whereas words spoken with kindness and compassion form beautiful crystals, radiating much light.

During one of Dr. Emoto's presentations, someone in the audience told how they had cooked some rice and placed it in two identical containers. Then the person talked to the rice every day. To the rice in one container, the person said, "Thank you;" to the other, "You fool."

The individual's two elementary school children also talked to the rice every day when they arrived home from school. As a result, the rice the children had said "Thank you" to was nearly fermented and had a nice mellow malted-rice aroma. The rice in the other jar, to which the children had said "You fool," had turned black and rotted. They said the smell was disgusting beyond description.[2]

After reading about this story, I cut out two photos from Dr. Emoto's book, laminated them, and placed them beneath my water pitchers. I chose the photos showing the effect of saying "I love you" and "I am grateful." I knew that the resonance signatures from the photos would transfer to my drinking water, thereby extending that beautiful energy to the cells in the body. If you haven't seen Dr. Emoto's water crystal photos, please consider exploring his impressive work.[3]

Simply hearing about the benefits of blessing our food and water isn't generally enough to motivate most of us to actually follow through. But once our mind registers this truth in picture form, we become inspired to take action.

Bob, who was a department manager at the water treatment plant, taught me a lot about working with people. It wasn't what he said that impressed me, it was his management style. Unless a major issue arose, Bob preferred a hands-off approach. He helped our HR department hire qualified water treatment operators, trained them in the basics of our treatment processes, and then gave them freedom to operate the treatment plant as they felt best. Visitors often commented on the relaxed working environment at our plant. Bob was extremely well-liked.

One day, a co-worker asked me if I knew why Bob paused in front of the doors of the treatment plant each morning before entering. It was the first I had heard of this practice. The operator no doubt noticed my puzzled expression.

"Bob pauses at the door to bless the treatment plant and the water that we treat," she explained with a smile.

When Oi and I first started blessing our food and water, I told her about these two heroes of mine. She asked me if I had told Bob how much I admired him and how his blessing of the water inspired me. At times, I had even paused to imitate his blessing at the treatment plant door. Upon hearing about his morning ritual from my co-worker, I had mentioned to Bob what a thoughtful gesture his blessing had been. Now, as he prepared to retire, I decided to call him and express my gratitude for all he had taught me.

Like Bob, Oi and I choose to keep things simple. While we sometimes expand on the following version of our blessing, this is our favorite phrase:

"We bless this food with love and gratitude in the name of the Inner Teacher, Divine Spirit, and the Voice of HU. Thank you. May the blessings be."

It has been my experience that, from a human perspective, gratitude often stems from comparing two similar situations. Gratitude can be used to measure what we are now experiencing against prior times which weren't as pleasant. For example, I remember sitting in my old jalopy waiting for a tow truck to arrive. I feel very grateful to now have a dependable car. From a higher perspective, however, we can rise above comparisons and feel grateful for all that life brings.

Appreciation often applies to that which we do not own. For me, appreciation involves looking at a situation from the Soul perspective, without comparison. It is more of an unconditional view of life. I am *grateful* for a sunny day because I have experienced clouds; however, I *appreciate* the sky. I have never struggled to own the sky or wished for sky to appear in my life. It has always been with me.

Sometimes, when I'm feeling especially connected with nature, I express my appreciation for a peaceful pond, a shady tree, or a mountain capped with snow. I use a similar blessing as with food but substitute the word appreciation for gratitude. Both gratitude and appreciation are valuable keys that open the door to love.

Recently, Oi reminded me about another important form of appreciation, one that many of us tend to overlook—self-appreciation.

Self Appreciation is a Spiritual Exercise by Pichaya

When Mike and I paused to admire a giant Oak tree near the ponds where we usually walk, a new spiritual exercise suddenly occurred to me. We had been discussing self appreciation at the time. I remembered a dark period in my life when I lacked self-confidence, had very low self-esteem, and felt unworthy of love. I asked the Inner Teacher, "How can I learn to love and appreciate myself more?"

The Teacher responded: "Self appreciation is recognizing your own greatness and knowing your true nature. You are a drop from the Ocean of Love and Mercy, here to expand your capacity to love."

With the limited view of myself, I could not imagine how a tiny acorn could grow into a giant Oak. I did not see myself as worthy of love and could not think of anything that I appreciated about myself. "Please tell me what *you* appreciate about me," I asked the Inner Teacher.

I was told three things: that I was a loving mother, a caring teacher, and a trusted life coach. I was guided to write these down in a journal and expand my list by one item each morning after contemplation. I did not know at the time that the Inner Teacher had shown me the first three branches on my tree of self appreciation. It would be up to me to add smaller branches and healthy new leaves, one by one, until the acorn had grown into a mighty Oak.

In a recent early morning contemplation, I was given three essential keys to help us grow our trees of self appreciation—by seeing, knowing, and being. First, we *see* ourselves through the eyes of love, eliminating all self-criticism and negative self-talk. We recognize our own magnificence and focus on our strengths. Secondly, we *know* our true identity as eternal beings beyond the physical form. Lastly, we practice *being* the HU.

For Mike and me, giant Oak trees are symbols representing self appreciation. Now, gazing up at the giant Oak, I am amazed at how far I have progressed. No longer do I engage in self-criticism or negative self-talk. Limiting beliefs and misconceptions of myself—like fallen leaves—have been replaced by fresh new buds.

Acorns tell us that it takes time to grow spiritually. It is important to be kind and patient with ourselves. Whenever we visit the giant Oak, we remind ourselves to appreciate who we truly are and how far we have travelled on our journey of Soul. Most significantly, we remember to express our appreciation for the Inner Teacher's nurturing love.

An Exercise in Spiritual Refinement by Pichaya

Another exercise involves putting our whole heart into everything we do. For me, this means being willing to go the extra mile in serving life with pure love *every* day.

When Mike stopped drinking goat milk, it was time to search for a replacement. Homemade almond milk seemed to be the best option because it is free of gluten, dairy, soy, sugar, locust bean gum, gellan gum, or any other kind of gum. After researching on the Internet, I found one recipe that had been given a five-star review.

The recipe suggested the following steps: Soak raw almonds in purified water overnight; mix each cup of rinsed almonds with four cups of water; add one teaspoon of vanilla extract and a pinch of salt; blend it in a high-speed blender for two minutes; then, strain, squeeze, and enjoy the creamy taste of almond milk. I followed the instructions, but only used three cups of water for a creamier consistency. When Mike tasted the milk, he commented how rich and flavorful it was compared to the ones we had purchased from the store.

The second time around, an important message was revealed to me while practicing the presence of the Inner Teacher at the kitchen sink. As I was washing almonds in a large bowl of purified water and rubbing them together in my hands, I noticed that the skins started to fall off. I then began peeling the almonds one by one. According to the recipe, it is unnecessary to remove the skins.

However, the Inner Teacher had a better plan. "If you can remove one, you can remove all," he told me. "To grow into mastership, you must become spiritually refined."

Suddenly, I realized that the almond skins symbolize negative thoughts and critical self-talk. They also represent toxic emotions such as anger, guilt, fear, worry, and doubt which prevent me from moving forward spiritually. My thoughts at the time were on my father. Being haunted by guilt, I was berating myself harshly for not being there physically when he made his transition.

As I noticed the color of the water turning muddy brown while rubbing the almonds together, the Inner Teacher whispered, "A polluted mind is contaminated by negative thoughts. Put your full attention on the sound of *HU* and fill your heart with love."

I then shifted my focus away from guilt and placed my full attention on my love for the Inner Teacher. Thirty minutes later, with the skins removed, the pearly white almonds were ready for blending. After completing the whole process, I asked Mike to taste the milk. Not only did he like it, he loved it. Although blanched almond milk requires additional time to prepare, it is absolutely worthwhile.

Spiritual refinement has become a rewarding family activity for us. When Mike observed me peeling almonds as a spiritual exercise, he asked if he could try it. I am now happy to report that Mike enthusiastically peels three cups of almonds two times a week—nearly a thousand almonds—which takes him approximately twenty minutes each session, the perfect length of time for contemplating and developing patience.

From my experience, the milk tastes sweeter when Mike peels the almonds. We both enjoy this exquisite creamy beverage in our favorite strawberry smoothie that Mike cheerfully prepares for us each afternoon. Through an exercise in spiritual refinement, the Inner Teacher has inspired both of us to go the extra mile for the richness of love.

Show Me Love by Pichaya

One morning, I was guided to experiment with a spiritual exercise called "Show Me Love."[4] It is simply to ask God to show you truth, wisdom, understanding, or love. For a whole week, I had been struggling with a minor conflict with someone and contemplating on finding the best way to resolve the issue with greater spiritual awareness and grace. I sang *HU* for a few minutes and asked the Inner Teacher inwardly to show me love. Then, I heard the Inner Teacher's voice. "Go to the park, now."

I knew he wanted me to go to the popular park where I frequently visit for five-mile hikes and bird watching. I usually start at the river where I look for eagles and hummingbirds before hiking the trails. However, on this particular day, I was guided to skip the river and go straight to the woods. In my heart, I knew that something was waiting for me, maybe a cute little puppy with a wagging tail and adoring eyes. This might be the way the Inner Teacher would teach me more about love.

After I had walked for nearly a mile, I noticed a woman sitting on a bench in front of me, twenty feet away. In her hands, she was holding a beautiful bouquet of roses—red, yellow, pink, white, and orange. She was crying.

I stood still, took a deep breath, and quietly asked, "Are you okay?"

She shook her head and said, "No."

I wondered what to do next. *Should I leave her alone and mind my own business?*

A few moments later, I was guided to ask the woman, "May I sit with you?" Without saying a word, the woman looked up at me and nodded her head. I stepped forward quietly and sat down beside her.

I broke the ice. "Those are beautiful roses."

She sobbed. Then, with a quavering voice, she uttered, "It is my husband's first anniversary." She pointed to the bench where we were sitting. It was built in memory of her husband.

I reached out my hand and gently placed it on her arm. After a long period of silence, I said in a comforting voice, "I am very sorry."

This time she cried even louder. I couldn't help but pull her closer, embrace her, and let her cry on my shoulder.

A few minutes passed. When she stopped crying, I continued: "I understand what you are going through. I have been there, too. I lost my first husband in 2001 when he died of lung cancer."

With curiosity, she questioned, "How long did it take for you to grieve?"

"A very long time—years," I answered. "Please take as much time as you need. His love for you will never die." After sitting quietly for a while, I asked if she would like to have my phone number in case she needed to talk. The woman reached into her purse, took out a pen, and wrote down my name and phone number.

Before we parted, she thanked me and spoke softly, "You are a godsend."

As I continued my walk, it felt as if my feet were floating above the ground. My heart was overflowing with joy and gratitude. Through me, the Inner Teacher had touched another Soul and had shown me love in an unexpected way. I thought I would be greeted by a puppy; instead, I was serving as a channel to share love with someone who needed it more. My minor challenge became insignificant. The heaviness in my heart lifted when the Inner Teacher answered my request, "Show me love."

We find that creating our own spiritual exercises can be an exercise in and of itself. By asking the Inner Teacher to accompany us on our spiritual adventures, we can access new frontiers. The exercise we've chosen to end this chapter was inspired by one of Mike's favorite poems, "The Bridge Builder," by Will Allen Dromgoole.[5]

The Bridge to Sach Khand

Imagine the Inner Teacher standing on the far side of a newly constructed wooden bridge. He has built this bridge for you to cross over into the Soul Plane, the entrance of a larger realm sometimes called *Sach Khand*. Listen to the sound of the rushing current below and marvel at the width of the chasm through which it flows.

As you grasp the Teacher's hand and step into Sach Khand, feel the love permeating this region. The single note of a flute calls to you from a distance. Now, thank the Inner Teacher for building this bridge especially for you and follow him to the Temple of Param Akshar.

- 6 -

IN SEARCH OF TRUE NORTH: HEALING WITH HU

"I have given this exercise to hundreds of people, and the results are phenomenal. For the next month, say over and over to yourself, 'I approve of myself.'"

—Louise Hay
You Can Heal Your Life [1]

Besides mastering patience, living with joy tops my priority list. I discovered early in life that unhappy individuals would prefer that others suppress their joy when around them. My father taught me this.

When I was five, I came into the house from playing outside on a sunny afternoon exuding joy. I was met by my father's scowl of disapproval. My happiness seemed to upset him. I didn't understand why, but after this incident, whenever I stepped through the door, I would make sure that my father didn't catch me laughing or smiling.

My father rarely spoke about his troubled youth and how difficult his life had been. He left home at the age of fourteen and struggled on the streets to survive. Joy was mostly out of my father's reach during his life, although he excelled in sports and was an avid fisherman. He found a small measure of happiness through these pastimes. Nonetheless, the judgment I formed from the incident with my father was carved deeply into my young and tender heart, much like the initials someone had engraved in the Laurel tree on the hill above our house: "If I express joy, my father will be upset." This judgment followed me down through the years like a cloud threatening to block out the sun.

Recently, I had a breakthrough which happened unexpectedly while contemplating on the events of my childhood. I am amazed by how the Inner Teacher speaks to us daily through waking dreams including the words of others, even songs.

Sawyer Brown

Before Sawyer Brown became famous, they always stopped at the Douglas County Fair near my hometown on their whirlwind summer tour throughout Oregon and the Northwest. I still remember how sparse and unruly the crowds were at times. You could always count on Sawyer Brown to be at the fair, rain or shine. They always showed up, whereas other bands cancelled smaller venues such as ours at the drop of a hat. I admired Sawyer Brown for that. When I left the fair each year after hearing them play until well after midnight, one song always stayed with me—"The Walk."

While contemplating on how to rekindle the joy I had expressed so freely before the incident with my father, I asked the Inner Teacher if there was anything from my past that I needed to resolve. Nothing seemed to happen during my spiritual exercise as I sang *HU*, but when I entered the kitchen, Oi's domain, I found myself humming my favorite Sawyer Brown song. As I was replaying memories from those carefree "Summer Fair Days" in my mind, Oi asked me if I realized that the Inner Teacher was sending me a subtle message through the song. It was no coincidence that "The Walk" had come to mind, seemingly out of the blue, right after singing *HU* for twenty minutes and asking the Inner Teacher for guidance. The song is about the relationship between a father and his son.

I located the song on the Internet and played it repeatedly with my own father in mind. After the sixth time, I experienced a shift in consciousness. I was able to view my relationship with Burt, as he preferred to be called, through the eyes of compassion rather than criticism. I knew that the root cause of my issue traced back to a prior time when I had caused others to suppress their joy. Yet, still, a part of me blamed Burt for shutting down my expression of joy in this lifetime. I had never really forgiven him.

With tears rolling down my cheeks, I saw scenes from our past through older and kinder eyes. I felt compassion for Burt's difficult life and forgave him for any hurt he had caused me. My father loved baseball and expressed his love by throwing batting practice until his arm gave out or darkness set in. He was always there for us, ready to fight anyone who dared mistreat his two boys. Even when he was diagnosed with cancer, his first thoughts were about taking care of his family. Like Sawyer Brown, you could always count on Burt. He always showed up, rain or shine. I admired him for that. I truly loved him for that.

Forgiveness healed my heart and opened a door that I had unknowingly kept closed with my criticism of my father and feelings of disappointment surrounding our relationship. With the release of emotions, coupled with gratitude for all Burt had done for us, I felt compassion for this great Soul who had taught me so much about the wonderful game of baseball. My heart opened to joy once again.

*   *   *

The Golden Blanket of HU

I'd been contemplating on a blood-sugar issue and had begrudgingly changed my diet yet again. Just as we awaken in stages, so do we heal in stages. Louise Hay wrote a popular book called *You Can Heal Your Life*. Her work explains the deeper causes of human ailments beneath the level of physical symptoms. According to the author, emotional trauma and limiting judgments are the soil from which physical problems sprout.

Chasing shadows on the ground won't change the shape of the Oak branch waving in the breeze above us. Addressing the source is the better approach. In my case, a lack of self-love appeared to be the hidden cause beneath a painful judgment: "I don't deserve the sweetness of life."[2] The body was only responding to the mental/emotional program.

Our answers often come from within, but sometimes we're directed to a specific healing modality or, in this case, a book. I was carrying a lot of guilt and sadness from a previous life when I had abandoned those I loved and, in turn, had been abandoned myself. At the time, I was unaware of how thoroughly Soul learns Its lessons by experiencing both sides of the polarity coin.

I took inventory: *Guilt?* Check; *Fear?* Yes, sir! *Anger?* A little; and a debilitating judgment stemming from being abandoned: "I am unworthy of love."

While I had addressed most of these deep emotional issues and had taken full responsibility for their creation, I was still carrying "sandbags of negative emotions" that were keeping my hot air balloon from leaving the ground more than a few feet.

It never hurts to ask, so I contacted the Inner Teacher and requested insights into the next step in my physical healing. I was given this spiritual exercise which took on a life of its own.

I imagined myself standing next to the Inner Teacher in the basket of a hot air balloon. Tethered to my belt loops were ropes connected to heavy sandbags lying in heaps upon the ground outside the basket. They were marked with big black letters: Guilt, Fear, Anger, Sadness, "I'm not worthy of love," and, "I don't deserve the sweetness of life."

With a smile of understanding, the Inner Teacher observed, "When we sing *HU*, the bindings that keep us earthbound loosen a little at a time. At some point, we gather all the lessons from our experiences and the ropes become thin enough to cut easily. You no longer need these weights that are keeping you from rising higher. You've done your part. Now, allow me to do mine. Do I have your permission to cut the ropes?"

"Yes, of course," I answered. "Thank you." I could feel the serenity and freedom the instant we lifted off the ground. I marveled at the view, as we rose higher and higher. But the air was very cold.

"I brought this from the Sanctuary," the Inner Teacher announced. He removed a soft golden blanket from a knapsack that was resting in the basket at his feet. "This is 'the Golden Blanket of HU.' It is spun from the purest strands of love. It was created by an unknown adept long ago to facilitate healing, and will serve as a reminder that you deserve the sweetness of life; most of all, the sweetness of love."

*   *   *

After sharing my hot air balloon experience and the Golden Blanket of HU with Oi, healing with love became a popular topic during Conversations with Honey. Oi remembers how the Dream Teacher provided love and support at an important crossroads in her life.

A Mountain Too High to Climb by Pichaya

"The only way out is through." It was the answer from the Inner Teacher, who appeared in a vivid dream one night in response to my request for healing. I had poured out my heart to the Inner Teacher expressing what had been troubling me for several months prior to this powerful dream.

The chronic depression, challenges with relationships, and suffering from Bulimia that I had been experiencing for over a decade, had become overwhelming. Twice before, I had entertained suicidal thoughts. Reaching my limit, I wished to leave this earth forever.

In my dream, I was walking through the Valley of Darkness. The night was long and full of terrors. I stumbled. I cried. I feared. I doubted that I would have the strength to carry on as I traveled this lonely path.

It was nearly dawn when the golden rays of the sun began to rise above the majestic mountain before me. The summit was higher than Mt. Hood in Oregon, which is approximately ten thousand feet in elevation.

As I drew closer, I noticed something strange about this peak. It was not decorated with green grass, colorful flowers, or glistening snow, but was covered with miscellaneous objects. Besides giant piles of junk food, there were dirty rags, old clothes, torn shoes, dented suitcases, and broken wooden closets. They looked familiar. Then it struck me; these objects had once been mine.

I was puzzled as to why my personal belongings had been scattered on this mountaintop. In the midst of my confusion, a gentle wind from the mountain blew softly in my direction. Instead of the delightful fragrance of wildflowers, it brought the putrefying stench of decaying waste. Suddenly, I realized that I was standing in front of a massive landfill. It symbolized my karma which had accumulated over many lifetimes.

For several moments, I stared intently at this towering mountain thinking to myself, "There is no way to go over, under, or around it." My heart sank. Feeling hopeless, I wept uncontrollably and fell to my knees. I punched the sharp-edged gravel with my fist. "I can't go on anymore," I shouted.

Then, I heard a familiar voice. "The only way out is through."

I looked up, and my eyes met the Inner Teacher's electrifying gaze. Tilting his head toward the mountain, he spoke compassionately, "You created all of this." There was no condemnation in his voice, only love.

I wiped my tears with my bleeding hand and asked, "How can I work off my karma?"

"Take full responsibility, serve life with love, and do everything in the name of the Inner Teacher," was his reply.

As I was awakening from my dream, the Inner Teacher reminded me, "Be assured of my love, for I am always with you until the end of time."

Serving Life with Love by Pichaya

The next morning, the Inner Teacher appeared on my inner screen during contemplation asking me to teach a Satsang class. Instead of embracing this honorable gift with an open heart, my immediate response was, "Who am I to teach? I am not good enough for anything."

"You are not the one who is teaching the class," the Inner Teacher stated. "I am."

The message was clear. I only needed to declare myself to be a vehicle for divine love and the Inner Teacher. Yet, fears of inadequacy held me back, which led me to question myself further: "How can I be a pure channel for love?"

I received an answer the following night. In a dream, while unlocking the door of the Spiritual Center where the Satsang class was to be held, something caught my attention. I felt a very warm energy radiating from inside the premises. Looking through the glass front door, I saw a spiritual teacher with whom I was familiar, Kata Daki, gazing directly at me. She greeted me with her beautiful smile as I entered the building.

"I have been waiting for you," she announced.

Feeling in awe of her loving presence, I was speechless. I responded with a smile and wondered what would be revealed to me next. Then, she led me to a table where a special book was located.

Kata Daki suggested, "Before beginning each class, open this book at random, contemplate, and listen for guidance from the Inner Teacher."

As the dream faded, I remember so clearly her compassionate voice. "A way to heal is to be of service to God," she stated. Kata Daki emphasized her final words with a loving smile: "Just Be Love."

Advice from an Adept about Healing by Pichaya

During the period of recovering from Bulimia, I diligently practiced a spiritual exercise called "The Sound Room."[3] In contemplation each evening, I asked the Inner Teacher to take me to a Temple of Golden Wisdom where the Sound Current of HU heals and purifies the inner bodies.

A series of dreams occurred over a period of several weeks. Each night, I found myself in a spacious room lying on a comfortable cot listening to the sound of a flute. A brilliant blue light shone down on me from a very high ceiling. During the healing process, I had the privilege of meeting an adept named Fubbi Quantz who kindly introduced me to a Paleo diet.

Fubbi offered these jewels of wisdom. "A lack of self-love is the root cause of Bulimia," he explained. "Know that you are worthy of love. Eat less, contemplate more, and discriminate between all things. Your diet should mainly be vegetables, fruits, nuts, and seeds, with a small portion of lean meat and some fish."

Since 2002, I have been following the adept's recommendations and learning how to take better care of the physical body—the temple of Soul—by practicing the virtue of discrimination. I have been making conscious choices to nourish the body with healthy organic food, along with regular exercise such as playing tennis and walking in the woods. Most significantly, I ended the cycle of binging and purging.

Through dreams, the Inner Teacher assured me that my karmic debts could be balanced one step at a time. My encounter with Kata Daki brought me a deeper insight on what it means to be of service to God. Following her instructions on how to conduct a class, I became more confident as an Arahata, a teacher, and joyfully facilitated Satsang classes for seven consecutive years.

Fubbi Quantz helped me understand the root cause of Bulimia. By taking full responsibility for what I had created in the past, by serving life with love, and by doing everything in the name of the Inner Teacher, I was able to love myself more and heal. As a result, I tasted the sweetness of spiritual freedom for the very first time.

*   *   *

Holographic Healing Rooms

Oi's experience in the Sound Room is similar to what I discovered during a morning contemplation. The image of an old friend came to mind while exploring some of the manicured grounds of the temple at Param Akshar. At least that was my first impression of him. But perhaps everyone here is an old friend. I'll call this Soul, Maurey, for ease of reference.

In my imaginative scene, I had stopped at one of the singing gardens where Souls congregate to enjoy healing music and socialize. Someone appeared to my right.

"Have you used any of the *HHRs*," Maurey asked casually. I found out that HHRs are *Holographic Healing Rooms*. It was the first time I had heard the term.

"No," I replied. "Please tell me more."

Maurey proceeded to enlighten me about the many "holodecks" available to those visiting from the worlds of matter, energy, space, and time. While Soul is perfect and complete in every way, the lower bodies often require healing and rebalancing. I had always been fascinated by the holodecks on the USS Enterprise of "Star Trek" fame. According to Maurey, he often visited a popular room where he would relax and rejuvenate.

He related that one could select from a nearly infinite variety of musical selections to accompany Light and Sound therapies. Technicians monitor and moderate the healing frequencies inherent in the musical waves which are carried by the current of love emanating from the heart of the Sanctuary.

Rather than musical choices, one may also request the sound of *HU* sung by a multitude and infused with divine love. It's difficult to explain, but somehow the body in need of balancing, whether physical, mental, or emotional, is projected in holographic form as part of the program. Images associated with the original cause of the imbalance are also at our disposal. Taking responsibility for having created the issue is the first step in the rejuvenation process. Maurey told me about other HHRs.

These were "Nature Park Rooms" (NPRs). Some were fields of colorful and fragrant flowers stretching as far as the eye could see; others were River Rooms, Forest Rooms, and even Ocean Rooms, where one could surf. How about an Orange Room, where every object is the healing color of orange? All rooms bathe the visitor in the most healing and loving energies. If these HHRs sound appealing to you, choose Option 2 on the Sanctuary Switchboard and ask the Inner Teacher to be your guide.

*   *   *

How could I have forgotten about Option 7? I wondered. I'd been thinking about the Sanctuary Switchboard spiritual exercise in Chapter Five. While many readers no doubt became excited about exploring Option 2: "To Request a spiritual healing," I found out later that Option 7 also relates to healing:

For directions to the Sanctuary, please press 7
The response was simply: "True North"

It was an intriguing answer, but where is True North? I wondered.

An impression formed into words within my consciousness: *"Search within. Go deeper and deeper. Finding True North holds an important key to your spiritual wellbeing."* The words came from the Voice of HU inside the Sanctuary.

Finding True North

Healing is all about love with a healthy dose of self-responsibility. A visit to the House of the Living Word further reinforced this truism. I stood before The Golden Book, soaked in the loving energies, and sang *HU* with reverence.

"How do I find True North?" I finally asked. "And how does True North relate to healing?" Familiar images danced into my consciousness.

Scenes from my working days at the Water District, where I'd served as the Accident Investigator for several years, appeared before my inner screen. *Root Cause Analysis* is a method employed to uncover the real issue which has caused an incident or an accident. One keeps asking the question, "Why?"

For instance, an employee backs into a tree and breaks a tail light. By asking why, we discover that the employee's truck had a broken passenger-side mirror, and the driver was unable to see the tree.

In our example, each month all employees are required to submit a checklist detailing the operating condition of their vehicle. Two months prior to the accident, the employee failed to fill out the inspection form and turn it in to his supervisor; therefore, the repair of the mirror was not scheduled. Ultimate responsibility falls upon the supervisor for not contacting the employee when the form was late. He should have asked for the paper work and reminded him that the procedure was written for the safety of all concerned. Had it been the vehicle's brakes needing repair, the situation could have been serious.

The supervisor might circulate a company-wide memo reminding all employees to fill out their vehicle inspection forms each month and turn them in on time. Any repairs could then be done expeditiously. This action might prevent a similar accident from happening in the future.

Root Cause Analysis can be applied to our personal lives as well. The cause of our health concerns and interpersonal issues can be more difficult to unearth since they often have deeper roots, originating in previous lifetimes. The Dream Teacher can show us these hidden causes through dreams, but we need to ask.

The Voice of HU then identified True North:

"While Magnetic North migrates around a pre-determined path in the Earth Realm, True North never wavers. Just as you can count on Polaris, the North Star, to always shine down from its fixed position, you can count on the Inner Teacher's love to be with you for direction and support; for healing if warranted. Let the Inner Teacher be your True North. He can accompany you here to this Sanctuary where love abides, if that is your desire. Ultimately, he can guide you back to the Infinite Ocean of Love.

"Know that many times it is possible to move beyond surface layers directly to the root cause which is an absence of love. Most health concerns trace back to either a lack of self-love or lessons of love to be gained from taking on an illness or challenge. Be kind to yourself. Utilize the spiritual exercises and send the love of HU into stressful situations and parts of the body starving for love's healing balm. Stay close to the Inner Teacher, True North, and ask him to show you love.

"The fountain in the middle of the pond where you walk with Oi represents self-love. Without that center, the ripples flowing outward so gracefully would not exist. Now, be at peace."

I'm beginning to understand how monumental finding True North has been for me. Surprisingly, I didn't fully recognize or appreciate what I had found for the longest time. I was always grasping for certainty, a permanent anchor point—True North—not realizing that the Inner Teacher has always been with me as close as my heartbeat.

- 7 -

OPENING THE HEART WITH HU

*"Your task is not to seek love, but merely to seek
and find all the barriers within yourself
that you have built against it."*

—Rumi[1]

Judgments from our past have a way of coloring our present life. They tell us in no uncertain terms that every new experience will be just like the ones from before. An outing at Bob's Red Mill Restaurant taught me an important lesson. A judgment about quinoa was the *plat du jour*.

Who Wants Quinoa Salad?
Over the years, I've practiced my share of unusual diets. Often, I have quinoa, flax seeds, and hemp hearts for breakfast. Fortunately, Oi loves spending time in the kitchen and makes homemade almond milk for my "cereal" as I call it. I've started drinking Chai tea with almond milk during Conversations with Honey as an alternative to coffee.

Several years ago, I ordered a quinoa salad for lunch at the urging of a friend. It was rather bland and tasteless. The other morning, Oi offered to make me a homemade quinoa salad. "It will be delicious," she remarked. "You will love it."

I wrinkled up my nose, at least inwardly, and replied, "No thank you, Honey." Undoubtedly, Oi's would have been much better than the salad from before, but, hey, it was quinoa salad.

Five hours later, I found myself at Bob's Red Mill Restaurant in Milwaukie, Oregon. I had dropped Oi off at a friend's house for a walking visit. It had been awhile since my last visit to Bob's where a wide variety of gluten free items are offered. But, now, as I walked back and forth past the large overhead lunch menu, I wondered if a single item would fit with my diet. Not even their gluten free bread was on my "safe" list. It contained Xanthan Gum. *HU-U-U-U-U-U-U-U-U.*

Then, lo and behold, in a refrigerated section near the hot-food counter, I spied something I could have, nestled among the seven containers I could not. It was—wait for it—quinoa salad!

When I told Oi about my delicious lunch on our way home, she observed, "What are the odds that I would mention quinoa salad, something you disliked in the past, and then you'd find it at Bob's among all the foods you couldn't have? The Inner Teacher takes care of us even in the smallest of details."

By the way, in addition to the three words everyone loves to hear—"I love you"—there are four more words that spouses enjoy hearing just as much: "You were right, Honey."

The following day, I asked Oi to prepare a homemade quinoa salad. It was fantastic. I learned a great lesson: Don't bring the past along with you on your journey to good health and an open heart.

Besides releasing past judgments, singing *HU*, and practicing the spiritual exercises, Oi remembers how the Inner Teacher brought her many opportunities for spiritual growth which inspired her to become a greater instrument of love.

The Transcendence of Love

The Sweet Song of HU by Pichaya

One of the most influential people in my life, the one who taught me how to open my heart, was my grandmother. From birth, she was always there for me, caring for me, nurturing me, and showering me with unconditional love. When I was beaten by life, she would lift me up and inspire me to become more. She encouraged me to view adversity as an opportunity to grow, reminded me to "do good karma," and to give without expecting anything in return. Most importantly, she emphasized, "Choose love above all else."

In the year 2003, I had to face one of my greatest fears: the fear of losing someone I love. I received an emergency call from one of my sisters in Thailand informing me of shocking news about our beloved grandmother. She had been in a coma for several days, and the doctor gave her seventy-two hours to live. My sister pleaded, "Everyone is here. Can you please come home now? Grandma is waiting for you."

My heart was shattered. Suddenly, the whole world seemed dark and cold. The intense fear of losing my grandmother, whom I loved completely, filled my weeping heart. I felt lost in a raging river of grief. With my trembling voice, I replied, "I will book the ticket tonight and see you all soon."

Immediately, I searched for flights from San Francisco to Bangkok hoping to be able to see my grandmother one last time. Unfortunately, there were no available seats either that night or the next morning; not even a first class flight. Feeling devastated with the situation, I sang *HU* and asked the Inner Teacher what to do.

I was then prompted to call the hospital and speak to my mother, who was sitting by my grandmother's bedside. "Please place the phone next to grandmother's ear," I requested. "I have something to tell her."

I spoke softly. "Grandma, I'm sorry I can't be with you now in person. Please don't worry, I am happy and well. Thank you for raising me, loving me, and believing in me. I love you so much and want to sing you a love song. Please be at peace." I sang *HU* for several minutes. Then, my mother asked me what I had said to grandma, because she had been crying the whole time.

"I told grandma I loved her and sang her a love song," I responded, wiping my tears.

"What is the name of the song?" my mother asked. "Can I sing it, too?"

"The name of the song is called 'HU,' and you can sing it, too." Through my tears, I demonstrated to my mother how to sing the sweet song of HU. Then we ended our conversation. A few minutes later, I received a call from my sister informing me about our grandmother's peaceful transition and her journey to a bright new world.

The Inner Teacher is always available to assist our loved ones cross the bridge during translation when we ask for help. Not only did the song of HU open my grandmother's heart, it also touched my mother's heart and brought serenity to everyone in the room. The song of HU gave me the strength to face my fear of loss. Yet, there were two more challenges waiting for me later that summer when a tiny creature appeared unexpectedly to teach me more about love.

A New Friend with Wings by Pichaya

At the age of seven, I was bitten by a street dog and, a few days later, scratched by a feral cat. Stray animals wandered around our neighborhood in a suburb of Bangkok and would attack people without warning. Fortunately, I was not infected with rabies, but the injuries were severe enough to traumatize me.

After those frightening incidents, whenever I encountered dogs, cats, or other animals that appeared friendly, I was still afraid to be near them. My phobia of touching animals followed me throughout my life until one hot summer day in the San Francisco Bay area, California. Once I had found the courage to embrace my fear, the Inner Teacher brought me a golden opportunity to heal.

My children were four, six, and eight at the time. After their swimming lessons, everyone was tired, hungry, and eager to go home. Racing toward our car parked under an Oak tree, Nate, the eldest, was a few steps in front of the rest of us. Something captured his attention. He stopped abruptly, then jumped up and down with his eyes wide open pointing to the ground. "Mommy, look! It's a tiny, cute, little bird," Nate shouted.

Approaching our newfound feathered friend, I studied it carefully and realized it was a premature, fledgling hummingbird, lying motionless on the burning concrete in one hundred degree heat. Its eyes were closed, and its beak was open. I looked around and noticed there were no shrubs or patches of grass nearby, only the Oak tree rising above the parking lot. "If I leave this baby here in this heat," I thought to myself, "it might not survive."

It is generally advisable to let nature take its course or contact a wildlife center, but I decided to sing *HU* and ask the Inner Teacher if there was anything we could do. Surprisingly, I received this answer. "Pick it up," the Inner Teacher directed.

My heart was racing as my stomach churned. My old fear of touching animals reemerged. I felt sick and knew that I would be unable to carry the baby with my shaky hands. I asked Jamie, my middle child, who loved all kinds of animals, to gently pick up our new friend and hold its delicate body in her palm. I announced to the children, "We are taking the hummie home."

During the twenty-minute ride, I sang *HU* in order to remain calm. Glancing in the rearview mirror, I saw Jamie beaming at the hummie with her compassionate eyes and heard her speak softly, "Go to sleep, little bird. I will sing you a lullaby." Jamie began singing "Twinkle Twinkle Little Star," and her siblings joined the soothing serenade all the way home.

"Let's sing *HU* to hummie," Nate suggested to his sisters. While I searched for an empty box, a soft towel, and some cotton balls for a temporary nest, my children sat in a circle on the kitchen floor and sang *HU*. After researching on the Internet how to properly feed baby hummingbirds, I filled a clean eye dropper with sugar water and placed it at the end of its beak while it rested motionless in Jamie's hands.

A few minutes later, we witnessed its long tongue reaching for the sweet nectar. It began to peep and blink feebly after a few drinks. Our jaws dropped, and our eyes were like saucers as we gasped in awe at the miracle that had just happened.

I gazed at this beautiful creature with a smile. When our eyes met, my heart melted. I could not help but fall in love with this adorable and delicate Soul. With my shaky hands, I extended my index finger and tenderly touched its head, then ran my finger down the length of its entire body to the tip of its toes. A warm wave of love flowed through me. My childhood fear began to dissipate and was replaced with the feeling of unconditional love for the baby.

I asked Jamie to transfer the hummie into the box and place it in her room. For the rest of the evening, I continued to feed the infant every twenty minutes until 10:00 p.m. Retiring for the night, I wondered, *What's next?*

Embracing Fear with Love by Pichaya

Early the next morning, the Inner Teacher brought us a wonderful surprise. I entered the girls' room to feed the hummie while Jamie and Caitie were still asleep. To my astonishment, not only did I find the hummingbird chirping and fluttering its wings, but it was happily swirling around the nine foot ceiling.

My heart was bursting with joy to see the baby bird regaining strength and becoming revitalized. I knew it was imperative to catch this tiny creature, put it back in the box, and return it to its mother. However, there was one challenge. In addition to my fear of touching animals, I was also afraid of heights.

I ran to the garage and returned with a ladder. On wobbly legs, I climbed up to catch it. After a few attempts, I was successful. With the baby in my hand, I felt its tiny heart beating rapidly. I then placed it in the box. Unfortunately, before I could close the lid, it flew out of the room and through the open back door which had, for some unknown reason, been left ajar the previous night. I found the hummie perched on the branch of a tall Oak tree in our backyard about twenty feet above the ground, chirping continuously.

This time I returned from the garage carrying a much taller ladder. I was determined to catch the baby bird and completely forgot about my fear of heights. My attention was fully focused on the love I was feeling for this beautiful Soul who remained motionless as I lifted it off the branch.

While my children and I were driving back to the pool, I sang *HU* and asked Prajapati, a spiritual teacher who cares for animals, to reunite the baby with its mother. Once there, we witnessed the hummie swiftly emerge from the box. It landed on a branch in the Oak tree—where Nate had first discovered it—and began calling loudly for its mother.

We surrendered the outcome to the Inner Teacher and drove home knowing we had done the best we possibly could to assist a beautiful Soul in need. This tiny creature of God inspired me to transcend both the fear of touching animals and my fear of heights, which allowed me to open my heart more to love.

* * *

The Open Heart by Pichaya

One of my favorite spiritual exercises is called "The Open Heart."[2] It involves loving or caring for some*one* or some*thing* more than we do ourselves. I practice this daily and have experienced a variety of profound results.

I love cooking and baking for family, friends, and neighbors. On one particularly crisp winter morning, I was given an opportunity to express my love to a stranger. As I was preparing to leave home to facilitate a Satsang class, I was guided to do something I would not normally do. In addition to the homemade chocolate chips cookies that I brought every month, I included a bunch of bananas and a $20 bill.

When I arrived at the Spiritual Center, I carried in the cookies but, for some reason, left the bananas in the trunk of my car. As I walked through the door, I debated whether I should go back for them. Then, the Inner Teacher whispered, "Leave them there." I followed the guidance but wondered, *Why?*

After our class had ended, my heart was fully open. I was grateful for our spiritual discussion and the time spent with friends. While walking toward my car, I noticed a woman about forty feet away, pushing a shopping cart. As she drew closer, I could hear the rattling of cans and the clinking of bottles. She greeted me with a genuine smile. Our eyes met, Soul to Soul. Pointing to my white faux fur coat, she exclaimed, "You have a beautiful coat!"

Immediately, I wanted to give it to her. I smiled back and asked, "Would you like to have it?" Her eyes lit up as she pointed to my favorite white faux-fur vest that I was wearing beneath my coat.

"I like this one," the woman said sweetly.

This surprised me. I thought she could really use my heavy coat to keep her warm since it was freezing cold. As I removed my coat and vest, I said to her, "If it fits, then it's yours." When she tried it on, it fit perfectly.

My heart danced when I saw the woman beaming as she ran her fingers through the furry soft vest. Thinking she could also use a winter coat. I offered mine to her a second time. "Would you like this coat, too?" I asked. "They go very well together."

"No, thank you." She shook her head and continued caressing her new vest as if she were petting a cat and hearing it purr.

All of a sudden, I remembered the bananas in the trunk and the $20 bill in my purse. When I offered her these gifts, she smiled broadly and exclaimed, "I love bananas. Thank you." I drove home floating on cloud nine realizing that The

Open Heart spiritual exercise is a powerful way to share the Inner Teacher's love with those I encounter.

Lunches and Lullabies by Pichaya

From kindergarten through high school, I packed homemade lunches for my children, including notes every day telling them how much I loved them. The lunches were mostly Thai food such as Pad Thai noodles, green curry, or fried rice packed in thermoses with loving care. Occasionally, I would send them to school with a variety of sandwiches, tortilla wraps, or chicken salad. In addition to a nutritious meal, there was a riddle or a joke and an inspirational quote about love.

Every night when they were small, I would spend fifteen minutes of quality time with each child reading stories and singing lullabies. They each had their own favorite stories and music. While Nate preferred English songs, Jamie and Caitie would rather hear me sing Thai lullabies. Before I kissed each child goodnight, we sang *HU* and expressed our gratitude toward life: "Thank you, God, for the house, family, and food." As I watched my children fall asleep in my arms, my heart overflowed with joy. I was grateful for the golden opportunity to learn how to love unconditionally.

Over the years, cooking for my children enabled me to become a creative cook and a talented baker. I learned how to prepare a variety of exquisite meals: Japanese, Chinese, Italian, French, and, definitely, Thai. When there was leftover food, I frequently combined the old with the new and created an entirely new dish, which I called "Medley." My secret ingredient is pure love.

My children—like tiny, fledgling hummingbirds—have left their nest and now live far away. I continually send them group texts with inspirational quotes and tell them how much I love them. I encourage them to ask the Inner Teacher and all the other spiritual teachers for help in times of need. Most importantly, I remind them, "Always remember to sing the love song of HU, the best lullaby of all."

Life is Better with Sprinkles by Pichaya

When I became a cat parent for JJ and Peaches, they taught me an important key to love. Besides following the golden rule, they urge me to revisit the platinum rule, a principle I studied when I was a professional life coach: Treat others the way they want to be treated.

In October of 2021, Mike and I discovered that our beloved cats were allergic to commercially manufactured food. We took them to see our friend, Ada, a naturopathic doctor, who specializes in Nutritional Response Testing. She suggested a raw food diet for immediate improvement and better health in the long run.

When a cat has grown up with kibble, such a radical change can be a challenge. I began researching homemade raw cat food on the Internet and studying how others had made the transition. Ada recommended placing crumbled sprinkles, which consist of crunchy, freeze dried chicken meat and organs, on top of their food in order for it to be more enticing. This small addition made the shift to a raw food diet a smooth one. I pointed out to Mike that it was a miracle.

JJ, the big brother and the Alpha cat, has trained me to be an outstanding server. In order to prepare his meal appropriately, it is necessary to apply a generous amount of sprinkles on top of his food. When JJ sees what he considers a small portion of topping, he will meow and give me a stern look that tells me, "I need more sprinkles, please."

Peaches, JJ's little sister, learned from her brother how to receive more sprinkles on her dish. JJ will have a few bites, then walk away from his bowl and wait for me to add more sprinkles. Observing her brother, Peaches will now step away from her bowl after a few bites, too. She looks at me disapprovingly with a question in her eyes, "Where are *my* extra sprinkles?"

Mike also loves sprinkles. When I included toasted, candied pecans made with vanilla, salt, cinnamon, and stevia in his quinoa cereal, he was pleasantly surprised. A minor addition can make a major difference.

Life is better with sprinkles—a loving hug, a gentle smile, a kind thought, and those three magic words, "I love you." They open our hearts and add sweetness to every golden moment. Unquestionably, the ultimate sprinkle is the song of HU.

- 8 -

BEING HU

"It is possible to live twenty-four hours a day in a state of love. Every movement, every glance, every thought, and every word can be infused with love."

—Thich Nhat Hanh[1]

Oi and I have heard and read "Be the HU" many times. We were even asked to facilitate a workshop on the subject at a future date. Since that invitation, we've spent considerable time reflecting on this topic during Conversations with Honey. This morning, Oi simply said, "Just be LOVE." That is how she lives her life. She makes it look so easy.

When I was playing baseball in college, I experienced what it feels like to be one with the ball. Fans would often marvel at how smoothly I fielded ground balls and how well I could hit. I imagine they chalked it up to natural ability, which is partially true, but I also spent countless hours on the practice field honing these skills. Fans weren't around in the early years to see me "boot a grounder." I paid the price for my modest success with bruises, scrapes, and blows to my ego.

To employ a baseball metaphor, when it comes to being the HU, I'm happy with my swing, but I still whiff at a curveball now and then. However, that's okay. I'm no stranger to the practice field.

In Oi's case, I know what she has endured to earn the right to say those three words that come so easily to her now: Just be LOVE. She has her own bruises and scrapes but doesn't complain. The following stories reflect Oi's commitment to serving the Inner Teacher and demonstrate what it means to "Be the HU."

A Quest for Love and Happiness

"Where Is Love?" by Pichaya

"Who am I? Why am I here?" As a very young girl, I asked these questions, desperately searching for the meaning of life. My aching heart was yearning to understand why I was experiencing poverty, injustice, and rejection, in addition to childhood trauma. Above all, I questioned, "Where is love?"

Seeking to find inner peace, I began practicing Buddhist meditation when I was six years old. I learned how to cultivate mindfulness by chanting Pali mantras and sitting in silence. During my meditation, I often saw a six-pointed blue star on my inner screen, but I did not know its significance until my early twenties.

When I first sang *HU* in 1994, I felt at home. I discovered later that the brilliant blue light in my spiritual eye was one form of the Inner Teacher, who had been with me since childhood. I also heard the uplifting sound of a flute during my quiet contemplation. I knew that I was on the right path, one which would lead to more peace, more joy, and, most significantly, more love. An important crossroads on my journey of self-discovery awaited me when I decided to leave the safety and security of my first career as a banker and step into the unknown.

Vice Principal by Pichaya

As I embarked on a new journey at a private elementary school in Bangkok in 1997, life taught me an important lesson about compassion. I was twenty-seven years old, impatient, self-absorbed, and inexperienced. As the new Vice Principal, I was fully engaged with daily administration, staff supervision, and teacher evaluations. In addition to implementing advanced learning programs, meeting parents, and disciplining students, I was also teaching English classes from first to sixth grade—forty children per class without a teacher's assistant.

There was a student in my second grade class who would constantly talk to other students during my presentations, using inappropriate language. He refused to listen to instructions and wandered around the classroom. The majority of my time was spent on disciplining him, which was a distraction for the other students who were eager to learn.

I became irritated with his continuous, disruptive behavior. Several weeks passed, and nothing improved. My exasperation reached the point where I was ready to resign.

Clearly, my strategy in teaching and managing the class was ineffective, especially when approaching the situation from a place of judgment, frustration, and intolerance. I felt discouraged and began to criticize myself harshly. Old stories replayed in my mind: "You are a complete failure and not good enough for anything."

Feeling overwhelmed, I sang *HU* and asked the Inner Teacher to show me how to resolve this student's behavioral issues. One day after my contemplation, I received a crystal clear answer: "He is a child of God. Treat him kindly as you would yourself."

I suddenly realized the core of this matter—self-perception. What I saw in my student was my own reflection. In order to properly reconcile this issue, it would be necessary to closely examine any negative thoughts and attitudes I held about myself. I would need to stop all self-criticism, judgment, and condemnation. In doing so, I would then begin to see my student through the eyes of love. Later that morning, I composed a letter and sent it to his family requesting a meeting in order to discuss the situation and hopefully find a mutually beneficial solution.

The boy's mother agreed to meet with me. As soon as she arrived, she broke down in tears and began pouring out her heart. She confided in me about her traumatic life circumstances. Listening deeply and attentively, I could resonate with the adversity that she and the boy had been going through. His experiences reminded me of my own when I was his age. I realized that he felt abandoned, craved attention, and needed love.

The parent meeting opened my heart and enabled me to see the root cause beneath his behavioral issues—primarily, a lack of love. In the following days, the Inner Teacher reminded me to utilize positive reinforcement, focus on his strengths, look for his goodness, and praise him when he did well in class. As a result, he was more polite and respectful toward me. He became more engaged in classroom activities and began to complete every homework assignment on time.

From interacting with this boy, I discovered the importance of cultivating self-love. When I approach life with kindness, patience, acceptance, and understanding, not only does it allow me to connect with others at a heart-to-heart level, it also empowers me to recognize the divinity in every*one* and every*thing* including myself. Compassion begins at home.

The New Girl by Pichaya

After raising three beautiful children, the winds of change brought me to a special place where I learned how to become a better lover of life. I once had a prestigious job at a school, and now I was being introduced as the new girl at the age of forty-seven. My task was not supervising others, but serving food, mopping floors, and occasionally washing massive stacks of dishes. I wondered, *How did I arrive here in an assisted living facility working with teenagers in the kitchen?*

Because I was raised mostly by my grandmother, I have always had a soft spot in my heart for seniors. It was natural for me to interact with the residents who loved telling stories about their lives. Serving those wonderful, shining Souls made my heart sing.

I spoke to them with respect, listened with love, and served with a smile. I felt connected to the residents, some more than others. Many of them adopted me as their granddaughter, and I loved them as my grandparents. I knew that life had brought me here to expand my capacity to love and, most significantly, to be the HU.

"Just Be Love" by Pichaya

On my way to work each morning, I declared myself to be a vehicle for divine love and the Inner Teacher. I was determined to do my best to make the residents feel loved and special. Each interaction taught me to appreciate the fleeting gift of life. I was guided by the Inner Teacher to make every moment count and serve life with love in an environment where kindness and compassion are especially needed.

I paid attention to every detail in terms of food, dessert, salad dressing, and their favorite flavor of ice cream. I journaled every experience and valuable lesson learned from those I served. When new residents arrived, I welcomed them with a smile and told them, "I'm happy to serve you."

Many residents asked me to visit them after work. On my days off, I would bring them flowers and homemade chocolate chip cookies along with a bag filled with multiple bottles of colorful nail polish. Pink was the most popular choice. Sometimes, I would play my guitar and sing for them. Mostly, I simply listened.

There was one resident named Marilyn who loved telling me about her life before moving into the facility. Her fondest memories revolved around love. Her eyes always lit up when she talked about the joy of raising her two beautiful children to become happy and successful individuals. She was a proud mother and inspiring college professor who touched the lives of her students in many meaningful ways.

Marilyn drove an electric scooter. Every time we met, she would reach her hands up in the air, arms open wide, and ask me to embrace her. "Can I get some vitamin H from you?" she would request. We both knew the importance of loving hugs, especially during the holiday blues when her son and daughter were absent from her life. She missed them terribly and became more depressed as time went by.

"Music washes away from the soul the dust of everyday life." Marilyn loved music and often referred to this quote from the German poet, Berthold Auerbach, when we spent time together each night after dinner.[2] Marilyn and her ninety-two year old friend, Violet, would linger in the dining room, visiting with me while I cleaned tables, set up utensils, and prepared menus for the following day. The subject of music arose during our conversation one evening.

"Do you play the harp?" Marilyn asked.

"Yes, a little," I replied timidly.

"Harp is the music of angels. Will you play for me one day?" Marilyn requested.

"I promise," I assured her.

A few months passed, and Marilyn's health declined drastically. She was in hospice care. I would visit her after work and bring vanilla ice cream in addition to her special dish, cottage cheese with freshly cut fruit—pineapple, strawberries, and a banana. She appreciated that I remembered all of her favorite food. During one visit, she asked me again, "Would you play your harp music for me?"

I replied, "I will play one day. I have been practicing two songs for you, but I am not ready to play them yet."

"Why not?" Marilyn implored in a feeble voice.

I looked down at the floor, feeling inadequate. "I'm not good enough. I'm not a professional harpist. I play music by ear and don't read notes. When I am ready, I will play it for you."

"Have faith in love and believe in yourself," Marilyn told me.

One morning, a resident named Betty came to search for me in her scooter while I was in the kitchen preparing dessert trays for the residents. With a sad look in her eyes, she informed me, "Marilyn is dying." My heart sank. "You should go visit her," Betty strongly suggested.

In that moment, deep in my heart, I knew what I needed to do. However, in my mind, there were fears, doubts, and self-judgements telling me that I was not good enough to play my harp for Marilyn. Then, I heard the Inner Teacher whisper, "Just be love."

That night after work, I drove home, picked up my harp, and returned to see Marilyn. I gently knocked on her door and entered the room on tiptoes. "Oi's here, Miss Marilyn," I announced. "I'm here to play my harp for you." There was no response.

She was sleeping in her bed, breathing slowly, with an oxygen tank by her side. I played "Oh Shenandoah" and "What a Wonderful World," two of her favorite songs that I had been practicing for the past several months.

Before departing, I had a nudge to play the HU song on my phone for twenty minutes while holding her hand, stroking her delicate blonde hair, and allowing love to flow through me. Then, I gave her a hug and a goodnight kiss on her right cheek. A few days later, she made a peaceful transition.

I am grateful for the Inner Teacher's guidance, reminding me to just be love. As a result, fear of inadequacy was replaced with an immense love which enabled me to find the courage to open my heart and give the gift of music to Marilyn—a promise kept. Most importantly, I had an opportunity to share the song of HU, which washes away the dust of everyday life.

The Secret of Happiness by Pichaya

There is no greater joy than being an instrument of love and making this world a better place for someone with a small act of kindness such as a smile. Working at the assisted living facility made me feel happy and useful. I treated the residents, who deserved the best possible service and great respect, as VIPs.

A resident named Clara remarked multiple times how she appreciated me being there. Her strict diet only included vegetables, fish, and eggs. On the days when these were not on the menu, I would ask the cook to prepare a special meatless meal for Clara. She often stated, "Thank you for your service. I appreciate that you really care for us."

One day, a gentleman joined her for lunch. As always, I greeted everyone in a cheerful manner before taking their order. Clara introduced me to her brother. "This is Oi. She serves with a smile," she praised.

I beamed at Clara's brother who commented, "I have heard a lot of great things about you. You always smile. What is your secret of happiness?"

I replied, "My secret of happiness is gratitude. I count my blessings every day. The more I count them, the more I find. I make a conscious choice to be happy in the moment. When I serve the residents, I am fully focused, even when I have challenges in my own life." At the time, I was facing life and death situations involving two of my loved ones.

Clara's brother then responded, "Your secret of happiness is gratitude. I can use the tip. Thank you."

Fast forward to December, 2020. My mission at the facility was now complete. I had learned many spiritual lessons in those three significant years—patience, compassion, tolerance, detachment, contentment, discrimination, and humility. It was fascinating to me how the ending of this cycle was in divine, perfect order. When I contracted COVID-19, I knew it was time to begin the next chapter of my life. I resigned from my position as a server and began writing with Mike.

Observing the residents decline and ultimately leave their loved ones behind, I learned two essential lessons: Life is all about *love*; it is also about *now*. I am forever grateful to those who touched my heart so deeply and taught me the value of living life to the fullest with love, joy, and service. Without the experience at the assisted living facility, I would not have realized the importance of embracing every precious moment.

Simple Ways of Being HU

A Smile by Pichaya

Being HU includes a loving hug, a gentle touch, a listening ear, an open heart, and a small act of kindness. Even a friendly smile can brighten someone's day. There is a park where I frequently walk near the Willamette River in West Linn, Oregon, bordered by thousands of beautiful trees. Dedicated volunteers keep it immaculately neat and pristine.

After contemplation one morning, I was nudged to go to this park. As I walked along, I thought to myself, "If I see any of the volunteers, I will definitely stop and tell them how much I appreciate their service to life."

A few minutes later, I noticed a park volunteer adding fresh bark chips to the path before me. I had seen him regularly, pulling weeds, picking up litter, and clearing brush with his tractor, but failed to express my appreciation in the past. This time, I acknowledged him with a smile and spoke in a cheerful voice, "Thank you for making this park so beautiful."

I completed a two mile loop and noticed the same man with whom I had interacted earlier. Once more, I greeted him graciously and remarked, "Hello again. Have a wonderful day!"

"Thank you for your smile," he responded, "You brightened up my day."

A Hug by Pichaya

The Inner Teacher always leads me to the right place at the right time to meet the right people in order to become a greater instrument of divine love. The key is to pay close attention to the inner guidance moment by moment, even when it seems incomprehensible and illogical to the analytical mind. When I follow a subtle nudge, the Inner Teacher can touch someone's heart profoundly, through me, in many amazing ways.

It was around Christmas time, and the grocery store was fully packed with impatient shoppers. One of those customers who felt irritated with the long lines at the checkout stands happened to be me. While silently complaining, I received a specific message from the Inner Teacher, "Go to lane six."

Why was he telling me to go to the longest line which had three more customers than any of the rest? I wondered.

Nonetheless, I followed the inexplicable instructions. As I studied the face of my cashier, I heard the Inner Teacher whisper, "When it's your turn, ask her, "How is your day going?"

All staff members of this store are trained to greet each customer with, "Did you find everything okay?"

Before she could speak, I inquired, "How is your day going?" She looked at me with tears in her eyes and responded, "Not so good. I just broke up with my boyfriend."

I suddenly realized why I had been directed to her lane. "Can I give you a hug?" I asked the woman.

Stepping out from behind her check stand, she wiped her tears. With her arms open wide, she reached out to me. "Yes, please. I really need it," she sobbed.

Listening for the Inner Teacher's guidance is an essential key to being HU. By following the explicit instructions, I was able to share the Inner Teacher's love with this woman in the form of a hug. Besides a smile and a hug, a kind word can brighten someone's day and even change a person's life.

A Kind Word by Pichaya

Sometimes Divine Spirit brings people into our lives who need reassurance that they are worthy of love. Kind words can also nurture, uplift, and inspire others. More importantly, they can be an open door to a healing.

A friend whom I'll call Elizabeth came to visit because she needed to talk about her childhood trauma that has continued to haunt her. Starving for love, attention, and approval from others, she allowed herself to be drawn into abusive relationships which caused her heart to be broken multiple times. As a result, she had lost faith in love.

I listened intently. Looking into her eyes, I recognized my own pain and remembered the time when I had experienced a similar situation. As she began to cry, I reached out my arms and held her in silence.

A few moments passed. An inner nudge prompted me to speak as words began to flow: "You are beautiful and worthy of love. You have so much to give to the world around you, but you can't truly give to others when you withhold love from yourself."

With tears in her eyes, Elizabeth spoke in her trembling voice, "No one has ever told me that I was beautiful and worthy of love."

"Divine Spirit is telling you now." I replied.

It is out of character for me to express my opinion or speak about what I know. When friends or strangers approach me, generally I listen without giving advice. However, when I declare myself to be a vehicle for love, sometimes I am surprised at my response and how I interact with those I encounter.

The Inner Teacher was demonstrating the Law of Economy for the benefit of the whole. The Teacher's words of love, kindness, and encouragement were not only for Elizabeth, but for me as well. It was a reminder for both of us to always remember that we are loved beyond measure.

The Power Bank by Pichaya

After living for over half a century, I am now beginning to understand my true purpose for being here on earth. Besides serving life, the main reason is to continuously expand my capacity to give and receive love. Only by being completely aligned with divine love, can I truly realize my full potential as a co-worker with the Inner Teacher and, ultimately, a co-worker with God.

Opportunities to be a clear channel for the Inner Teacher are endless. They can present themselves anywhere, anytime, especially on planes. Strangers frequently open their hearts to me and share stories about their lives, mainly their relationships. My flight from Denver to Oregon proved to be one such case.

Flying back to Oregon from a trip back East on a snowy winter night, I happened to sit next to a young college student. While she confided in me about her challenges with school and her relationship, our conversation was interrupted by an announcement from the captain: "Due to adverse weather conditions, please remain seated."

As the plane began to wobble, I silently sang *HU* in order to remain calm. The young woman turned to me and asked with a panicked look on her face, "Are we going to be okay?" I reached out my hand and touched her forearm gently, but firmly, as screams erupted from passengers in the rows behind us. "We will be okay," I answered reassuringly, although I did not know this for certain.

The bumpy ride became even more intense. The young woman's face turned pale. My heart began to race as I felt the fearful energy spreading throughout the plane. In the midst of this crisis, I heard the Inner Teacher whisper, "Sing *HU*."

Circling above the frozen Portland airport runway, our captain announced that he was unable to land due to extreme icy conditions. Unfortunately, we would need to redirect to Boise and wait until it was safe to land at our destination. Many of us expressed our frustration at this unexpected turn of events. Some sighed, some moaned, and some complained, while we sat impatiently on a lonely Boise runway in the middle of the night for nearly an hour.

Silently, I asked myself, "What is the point in all of this? Why are we here in Boise?"

Just then, the young woman next to me asked if I had a power bank or a portable phone charger. Her phone had only one percent of battery life remaining. She said, "I will need to call my father to pick me up as soon as we land, but my phone is dying. Can I please borrow your charger?"

Fortunately, my power bank was sufficiently charged, and I was able to share it with her. Once back in Portland, we finally landed safely. As we departed, she thanked me again for listening and for allowing her to recharge her phone.

In retrospect, I realize that we are all power banks. In order for us to be fully charged, it is essential to be connected to divine love. The simplest way to build a strong connection and become a pure channel for this love is to sing *HU*. I also realized that my purpose for being on the plane next to this young woman was to be the HU.

Part III
The Universe *Is* HU

- 9 -

THE MANY MIRACLES OF HU

*"You are a Divine creation, a Being of Light who showed
up here as a human being at the exact moment you were
supposed to. You are the Beloved, a miracle,
a part of the eternal perfection."*

—Wayne Dyer[1]

If I could go back in time and give myself, as a young man, a sound piece of advice, I'd say, "The secret to being happy is in learning to recognize small miracles and in appreciating the beauty of an ordinary moment. Let the larger miracles take care of themselves, with the Inner Teacher's help of course."

Lots of miracles happen when we write a book, a screenplay, or compose a song. For instance, initially, we had a chapter in mind called "HU Heard 'Round the World." Following a subtle nudge, we replaced it with "Opening the Heart with HU." Once we made this change, the outer book matched its inner counterpart and the puzzle pieces fit together nicely. Oi sees this as a miracle of HU. I view finding her in this lifetime as another miracle of HU.

The Lonesome Monk and the Himalayan Princess

Once upon a time, a lonesome monk fell in love with a beautiful princess. I doubt that you've heard this centuries-old story set against the snow-capped mountains of Nepal, or was it Bhutan? How these star-crossed lovers met, fell in love, and struggled to conceal their forbidden romance, is a fascinating tale for another time.

Unlike the happily-ever-after endings to which we're accustomed, the monk in this story was banished from the land, and the Himalayan Princess lived out her days in isolation longing for her beloved. Sadly, this is how their storybook romance ended...or did it?

Years ago, I was flipping through television channels on a quiet Sunday evening and happened upon a documentary featuring a monastery located high in the Himalayan Mountains. I found the images on the screen strangely familiar, even captivating. A memory bubbled up from the depths of Soul, and I found myself observing a clear past life. To my astonishment, I had lived in this very same monastery and, as fate would have it, fell in love with a royal princess.

Unfortunately, I was so distracted watching this present-day documentary, while at the same time viewing scenes from my past, that I failed to write down the name of the monastery or even the country where it was located. By the end of the program, my emotions were raw. I felt a longing rise up from within my heart accompanied by a question: *Will I ever meet my princess again?*

Several years passed, and I forgot about the documentary and the scenes from so long ago. Then, one afternoon, my life took an unexpected turn. I was invited to a potluck where some friends of mine had gathered. I couldn't tell you the names of those in attendance; I only remember Oi.

She was greeting people at the door, standing in a ray of sunshine. Time disappeared, as I gazed once again into the eyes of my princess.

Oi probably wondered why I called her "my princess" when we began dating. It is a miracle of HU that we found each other again, two people living on opposite sides of the world. Now, we sing *HU* every morning and celebrate each moment together.

Growing up in Thailand, Oi discovered early on how to recognize small miracles: shoes of any kind to wear, some rice and salt for dinner, and a few hand-me-down clothes. Perhaps that's why she sees many things I take for granted as miracles. It is amazing to share my life with such a compassionate and aware Soul. I've learned a lot from Oi, including how to recognize the hand of the Inner Teacher in ordinary moments. To her, there are no ordinary moments.

* * *

Appreciating Water by Pichaya

Viewing the world with deep appreciation can help us open our hearts to the miracles in every moment. For example, when I was a teenager, I sometimes visited my aunt's house in a rural province where there was no electricity or access to piped-in water. Rain, wells, and a nearby river were the only sources available.

I helped her carry two buckets filled with water from a well half a mile away from her house using a long wooden stick balanced over my right shoulder. She stored it in large clay containers in her kitchen, bathroom, and on her crowded back porch. The water was discolored, and my aunt would boil it on her small clay stove using charcoal to make it safe for us to drink.

On the other hand, our family in Bangkok was fortunate to have had electricity and piped-in water. We purchased filtered water to drink from a nearby store. Since we didn't have a hot water heater or shower, in wintertime, we boiled water in a large pot on an old clay stove using charcoal for bathing. We used it sparingly and appreciated every single drop. Having access to running water was a miracle to me.

In 1994, I discovered another miracle—the ancient mantra called "HU." I began singing *HU* every morning as a spiritual practice which enabled me to establish my personal relationship with the Inner Teacher. This special connection with the Inner Teacher changed my life far beyond what I could have ever imagined. One day, it saved my life.

"Do Not Go to Work!" by Pichaya

"Do not go to work today." It was a warning from the Inner Teacher after my morning contemplation on June 14, 1995. At the time, I was employed by Bangkok Bank, located in the heart of Bangkok where it was congested with heavy traffic. Traveling by bus during rush hour, I would be packed like sardines in a tiny can. It would take up to two hours to arrive at work. The fastest way to commute was by ferry boat, followed by a motorcycle taxi. In order to avoid the crowd of a hundred other commuters, it was necessary to be at the Pran Nok pier by 7:30 a.m.

As I stepped out the door, the Inner Teacher cautioned, "Do not go to work today."

I thought to myself, "It doesn't make any sense." I ignored the inner voice and continued walking in the direction of the pier.

The voice spoke to me again while I was walking down a narrow street. This time, it was very loud and clear: "Do *not* go to work!"

Suddenly, I began to feel a strange sensation in my abdominal area to the point where it was too painful to continue walking. I curled up on the ground with my two hands holding my stomach. This discomfort lasted for several minutes. When I stood up, it felt as if some*one* or some*thing* turned my body around and gently pushed me back toward my apartment instead of the pier. Then, I remembered a similar warning when I had heard a voice telling me to refrain from a particular course of action in order to avoid unnecessary harm.

Once home, my neighbor told me about the tragic news he had heard on the radio a few minutes earlier. A ferry had crashed into the dilapidated old pier, resulting in at least twenty deaths and over thirty injuries. The event occurred at the exact time and place where I would have been waiting for a boat. Had the Inner Teacher not intervened, I could have been injured or even killed. This miraculous experience taught me the necessity of following the Inner Teacher's guidance in every moment.

"This is for Your Children" by Pichaya

Sometimes, a subtle nudge can lead to unexpected gifts. An encounter with a stranger in the San Francisco Bay Area of California is a perfect example. After contemplation one morning in 2004, I was guided to take my children to a specific park on a bright sunny day. At the time, they were two, four, and six years of age. Nate, my oldest, was at the stage where he was more interested in playing catch with me than sitting on a swing, going down a slide, or running around the park with his sisters.

Nate noticed a retail store nearby and asked me to purchase a ball. My reply was, "Not now. Why don't you run with your sisters or bake some yummy cheesecake for me?"

Nate loved playing with dirt. His favorite game was using his creative imagination to cook homemade gourmet food and make exotic desserts. However, on this particular day, he began to whine and insisted on going to the store for a ball. As Nate's whining persisted, I sang *HU* to soothe myself. *Wouldn't it be great to have a ball for the kids?* I pondered.

A few minutes later, I noticed a man standing about twenty feet away, to my right. He was wearing a blue cap, a blue shirt, and blue jeans. Walking toward me with a welcoming smile and shining eyes, he handed me a new blue ball.

He said kindly, "This is for your children." Then, he walked away and disappeared in a grove of trees leaving me wondering what had just happened.

Holding the ball in my hands, I felt as if my feet could barely touch the ground. My heart was overflowing with gratitude and dancing with joy. This memorable incident reminded me of previous encounters when strangers had appeared inexplicably, "out of the blue," to guide, protect, and offer help in times of need. Later, I realized that the man who had given me the new blue ball was an unknown spiritual teacher who had come simply to give us love.

Rebazar at the Helm by Pichaya

In 2015, when my children were teenagers, we went on an excursion to one of the most beautiful places in the world where I recalled a traumatic past life experience. Hong Island is situated in Krabi, in the south of Thailand. It is well known for its impressive limestone formations; turquoise blue water; and soft, white, sandy beaches. We were accompanied by my sister and her husband, who hired a skillful captain to cruise us around the exotic island on a private, wooden long-tail boat.

My sister and her husband went swimming and snorkeling with my children in the crystal water. I could hear their joyous laughter from the shoreline. Unfortunately, I did not know how to swim.

On our way back to Koh Yao Noi where we were staying, it began to rain. We were greeted by a howling wind and strong waves five feet in height, which caused our boat to rise and fall with each swell. Each surge brought up deep rooted fear within me. My heart was pounding as if it would escape my chest. My fifteen-year-old daughter, Jamie, started to cry. Her body trembled. With her eyes full of tears, she asked me, "Are we going to die here, Mom?"

The frightening situation brought to the surface a catastrophic scene from a past life where I had found myself submerged under the sea. As I recalled those dreadful memories, I suddenly felt suffocated and desperately gasped for air. With my shaky hands, I pulled Jamie into my arms and said in my quavering voice, "We have protection from the Inner Teacher and other spiritual teachers. Let's sing *HU* and ask for help.

Jamie followed my advice, and we both sang *HU* with tears streaming down our cheeks. I surrendered my fear as I spoke to the Inner Teacher inwardly, "I don't see this as our time to go, but if this is Your will, Thy will be done."

Meanwhile, we continued singing *HU* softly. With my eyes closed and Jamie in my arms, I imagined a powerful spiritual teacher named Rebazar,[2] and pictured him in a maroon robe as our captain standing gallantly at the front of the boat with a shining blue star as our guiding light and little people supporting us from beneath.[3] Jamie also called upon Lai Tsi, another spiritual teacher, who has appeared in her dreams since she was young. Our intense ride lasted for thirty minutes. Finally, we arrived safely on the peaceful shore.

My sister and her husband did not seem to be frightened by the stormy sea; neither did Nate nor Caitie. As a matter of fact, they reported later that the rocking boat reminded them of a thrilling ride called "The Jurassic Park River Adventure" at Universal Studios in Florida where they had been multiple times. Conversely, Jamie and I were triggered by harrowing past life memories of drowning in the deep blue sea.

I realized how we respond to life's circumstances—with love or fear—depends upon our individual states of consciousness. Our trip to Hong Island provided a wonderful opportunity for Jamie and I to utilize the power of creative imagination to cope with our fears. This experience also deepened our trust in the Inner Teacher who is here to assist us through the stormy seas of life and reassure us that we're never alone.

Warning: Coyotes by Pichaya

The Inner Teacher speaks to us constantly. He brings us love, guidance, insights, and protection through the voices of all living creatures. I often receive warnings in advance through dreams, waking dreams, contemplations, and inner guidance; however, I sometimes fail to recognize or understand the message.

During my daily five mile walk, I frequently meet Tim, a neighborhood friend. On one occasion, Tim asked me, "How far are you going today?"

"I want to go for eight miles," I replied with a smile.

Tim gave me a puzzled look and remarked, "That is a long walk." He continued, "The other day I spotted two coyotes running around." Tim could see concern in my eyes.

"They will not harm you," he assured me. "Don't worry. They are okay."

As I continued my walk, I thought about our conversation. *Why had he mentioned coyotes?* I wondered. I had never seen a single one on my previous walks.

With my eyes focused on the ground introspectively, a strong inner nudge prompted me to glance over toward the street on my left. Forty feet away, I noticed a man walking in my direction on the sidewalk. Not only was he looking directly at me with a snarl, he was also giving me an obscene gesture. This man began swearing and yelling angrily at me for no apparent reason.

It was a very cold, gloomy day, and no one was walking in my vicinity. With my heart racing and chills running down my spine, I began telling myself a fearful story: "This man can attack me, hurt me, or even kill me. He might have a gun or a knife."

The moment I caught these negative thoughts stirring in my consciousness, I was reminded by the Inner Teacher to sing *HU* and imagine a blue globe shielding me from the man's loathsome vibrations. Even though my instinct was to run, I was instructed to remain calm, continue walking, and send the man divine love.

After I had passed him, I could still hear his threatening voice filled with rage. I kept my full attention on the Inner Teacher's loving presence as I walked at a rapid pace and continued singing *HU* out loud. Fortunately, shortly after that, I arrived home safely.

I reflected back to my conversation with Tim who had given me a warning about coyotes, which represented this man. Messages from Spirit that sometimes come through spoken words are called "Golden-tongued Wisdom." Tim emphasized that coyotes would not harm me, and he was right. I realized that the man was mentally ill; otherwise, he would not have been acting in such an erratic way. By choosing to send him love, I was able to transcend the negative emotions of fear, blame, and anger. When confronted with a challenging situation such as this one, it is essential to place my full attention on the Inner Teacher and remember to sing *HU*.

"Bee" Careful by Pichaya

While contemplating on a story for the "Animals Love HU, Too" chapter, Mike and I ambled along a pebbled path beside a peaceful pond. We sang *HU* together as we appreciated the beautiful scenery—a dancing fountain, croaking frogs, and a couple of playful ducks preening each other. However, on this specific day, we were guided to choose a different route. Instead of proceeding along the pond, we turned right and continued our walk through a friendly neighborhood.

We noticed a sketch on the sidewalk drawn with colorful chalk, presumably by an aspiring grade school artist. It was an illustration of a yellow and black bee with the statement, "Bee careful." The moment we saw the image and the word "Bee," we instantly knew this was a confirmation from the Inner Teacher for Mike to write about our profound experience with a bee at this pond the day before. (This story appears in the following chapter.)

We were grateful for the information, however, the word "careful" caught our attention. *What is the Inner Teacher telling us through this cautionary message?* we wondered. *Could it be a prophetic warning about our writing, our lives, our health, or our loved ones?*

Paying close attention to a small nudge and following the inner guidance can help sidestep unnecessary harm. Unfortunately, neither of us knew the meaning of this seemingly important message from the Inner Teacher.

Sometimes the answer is not revealed until additional puzzle pieces appear in our lives.

A Giant Leap of Faith by Pichaya

A few days later, the mystery was solved. A stressful incident with Faith, our beloved car, reaffirmed my trust in the Inner Teacher and introduced me to a spiritual teacher with whom I was unfamiliar.

I was planning on going to a park after visiting a friend, but the Inner Teacher had a different arrangement for me. As soon as I started the car, an oil can symbol illuminated above the speedometer. I glanced over at the iDrive screen and read: "Engine oil pressure too low. Switch off engine. Possible engine damage. Continued driving is not possible."

Thinking this might be a false alarm, I asked inwardly for guidance and heard, "Go home." Apparently, it was dangerous to drive Faith in this condition, but I chose to rely completely on the Inner Teacher's assistance. I was hoping to arrive home safely and ask Mike to inspect it later.

My pulse began racing like a freight train. Suddenly, an image of a car catching on fire—one I had seen a few years before on a freeway—flashed in my mind. Being engulfed by fear, negative self-talk began to creep in as I imagined the worst case scenario: Faith might stop running in the middle of the road; she might catch on fire, or I might have a severe collision. The more I focused on these terrifying thoughts, the harder my heart pounded.

Glancing again at the warning on the screen—"Continued driving is not possible"—I felt frightened. However, at that moment, I recalled a phrase, "With God, all things are possible," and repeated the words out loud. In order to calm myself down, I began singing *HU*.

Then, I remembered a story about a woman's encounter with a spiritual teacher named Rami Nuri.[4] A pregnant woman had a flat tire on the freeway and discovered that her spare was also flat. Rami Nuri, driving a white Porsche, stopped and asked if there was anything he could do to help. After giving her a ride to a phone booth, he gave her his business card. When she called the Porsche dealership listed on the card a few days later, she was told that nobody by that name had ever worked there.

The Inner Teacher reminded me that spiritual teachers are here to assist in times of need. Consequently, I called upon Rami Nuri by chanting his name and asked him to accompany me. I sang *HU* the entire twenty minute drive and arrived home shaken, but safely. From this leap of faith, I experienced firsthand a miracle of HU.

A Spiritual Wake-Up Call by Pichaya

Once home, Mike discovered that the engine oil was extremely low. Usually, in the past, an indicator would inform us when it was necessary to add oil. For some reason, this warning did not register on the iDrive screen.

Mike purchased oil at a nearby auto parts store and taught me how to add it to the engine. I learned a new word, "dipstick." In addition, he thoughtfully placed a spare quart in the trunk along with a roll of paper towels and a jug of water in case of future emergencies. I appreciate how Mike goes the extra mile to show his love for me in everything he does. However, it is still my responsibility to take care of Faith, including checking the oil and scheduling routine maintenance.

Every time I experience car trouble, I know there is a significant message relating to my personal life. Symbolically, Faith represents my physical body, overall health, and wellbeing. It was critical for me to understand the deeper meaning of the low oil pressure warning. With curiosity, I did some research on Google. "What would happen if I drove a car without engine oil in it?" I asked. The answer: "Damaged and ruined Engine."

This experience was my wake-up call. I learned the importance of self-responsibility in taking care of my own health in addition to Faith. Since we both are aging, it is imperative to add more clean oil to our engines in order to operate smoothly. As a result, I began including more avocados in my diet and diligently taking essential supplements, but still not as many as Mike. He is still the champion.

In *Those Wonderful ECK Masters*, Sri Harold Klemp wrote about Rami Nuri. He stated, "The letter *M* appears on his forehead."[5] Mike believes that Rami Nuri helped him with Betsy, his Subaru Outback, earlier this year. We asked for a confirmation that he had also assisted me with Faith.

We received our answer the following evening while discussing the subject on a walk through an Oak grove. An inner nudge prompted me to look down. I smiled broadly, pointed to the ground, and exclaimed to Mike, "Here is our answer." There were four twigs arranged neatly into the a shape of the letter *M* on the path in front of us.

This powerful wake-up call inspired me to take better care of my health. Above all, I am grateful to the Inner Teacher and the other spiritual teachers for their love and protection. They have opened my heart to recognize and embrace the many miracles of HU.

- 10 -
ANIMALS LOVE HU, TOO

"Pets can teach us a great many things—patience, flexibility, how to live in the moment, how to laugh at ourselves. But most of all they can teach us how to give and receive unconditional love."

—Harold Klemp
Animals are Soul too![1]

Animals and birds sense the vibrations of HU, even when they are beyond the sound of our physical voice. Oi and I experienced this phenomenon recently. A stream meanders through a series of ponds where we walk most evenings. We've made friends with the crows, ducks, frogs, squirrels, a great blue heron, and a vulture, whom we call George. Fluffy the Crow and Chelsea the Ground Squirrel are my favorites. Oi won't choose a favorite.

Claire and "The Godfather"

We also enjoy watching a large black, grey, and white, well-traveled duck who always seems to be in everybody's business. If he's not chasing another duck with his head menacingly low to the ground, he, himself, is escaping from an angry mother duck who took offense at his unsolicited advice. We call him "The Godfather."

While reflecting on this chapter recently, Oi and I sat on a wooden bench overlooking a pond and sang *HU* quietly. We didn't direct our thoughts; we simply allowed the energy, consciousness, and the love of HU to flow through freely. I noticed a lone female duck floating in the water well beyond earshot range. I nudged Oi, as the duck began swimming our way, moving her head from side to side as if searching for something. Finally, Claire, as we named her, emerged from the reeds at the edge of the pond and cautiously walked up the bank in our direction.

Claire approached to within a few yards, looked up at us singing *HU*, and then returned to the water, apparently satisfied that she had located the source of the love she felt from across the pond. Oi and I thanked the Inner Teacher for confirming that a chapter on animals deserved a place in our book. I'm sure Claire would agree, with the Godfather's approval of course.

Ceremonies of Transition

Several years ago, a deer jumped down from the shoulder of the country road I was traveling and bounded out in front of me. There was no time to hit the brakes or swerve to avoid impact. Sadly, the doe lost her life. My car received minimal damage, which is rare for such mishaps.

I sang *HU* and asked Prajapati, a spiritual teacher who cares for animals, to help this beautiful Soul make her transition. While I had seen deer remains beside the road my entire life, I had never been involved in their demise. I felt horrible and relived the scene for days. But then, one night in contemplation, the Inner Teacher urged me to view this traumatic experience from a higher perspective.

I saw it as an honor to be asked to help this gentle Soul leave this world. Rather than a brutal accident, the incident was a sacred ceremony. At some point prior to the collision, I had agreed to play an important role in her transition. Feelings of remorse were replaced with gratitude and unconditional love. My heart opened wide. This experience foreshadowed a more recent event.

Oi and I followed an inner nudge to visit a small pond a few miles from the Godfather's domain. We hadn't been to this pond for quite awhile but always enjoyed watching bees dart from wildflower to wildflower gathering nectar this time of year. When we stopped to rest on a wooden bench overlooking a fountain, Oi noticed something unusual. She pointed to a bee crawling slowly toward us across the burning concrete path.

Once it approached Oi's foot, it turned around and started back in the opposite direction. "Why isn't this bee flying?" Oi asked with concern. "Is it sick?"

At this point, the bee rolled over on its side and could not get back to its feet. Its wild flailing caused it to flip over on its back. Oi used a leaf to transport it over to a shady area near some flowers. We picked an orange poppy, a red and white clover, and a tall purple flower, which seemed to be the flower of choice for bees in the area. Placing them around it, we asked for inner guidance as to what to do next.

"Sing the *HU* with love," was the response. "It will soothe the bee and ease its pain during translation."

Oi and I both understood the sacredness of this moment. It was now clear that our decision to drive to this pond at this exact time was a subtle directive from the Inner Teacher. Had we dismissed it, we would have missed an opportunity to help a fellow Soul during one of the most important moments of Its life. We were honored to sing *HU*, offer flowers, and represent the Inner Teacher in this Ceremony of Transition.

Shadow's Gift

I sometimes sing *HU* to the feral cat at the river where we feed jays and squirrels. Shadow loves attention as much as she loves the food people bring for her. I befriended Shadow more than ten years ago, when she was first abandoned, and fed her each morning while working at the water treatment plant adjacent to the park. Winters are especially difficult for Shadow. I grew to admire her survival skills and strength of will. She has been an inspirational teacher.

Shadow provides a wonderful service—she allows people to love her. Some of those frequenting the river have no other avenue for giving and receiving love.

A friend of ours named Sharon is an animal communicator who works with animals on the spiritual level. Once, while Oi and I were asking questions about JJ and Peaches, I happened to mention Shadow. To my surprise, a message came through from Shadow's Higher Self. She thanked me for singing that special song to her over the years—HU. It made her feel warm and loved.

Sharon related afterwards that all Souls recognize and respond to HU as a source of love and comfort, no matter what body form they inhabit. When I asked her for permission to include this message from Shadow in our book, Sharon told us more about the monumental role the HU can play in the lives of animals.

"HU Brings Us Home"

"Live above the words. Learn the HU as a bridge for Soul to go to the Light and Sound. The HU brings us home." These gems of wisdom came through from Leo the Lion, Sharon's cat, during his translation from this lifetime. He purred softly on the bed while Sharon's husband played the HU Song. As the recording ended, Leo the Lion made his transition peacefully.

After speaking with Sharon, I understood more clearly why Oi and I had been called by the Inner Teacher to the pond where the bee was in the process of translating. The song of HU is the golden bridge upon which Soul finds Its way to the Light and Sound. Sharon also gave us permission to pass along the following examples of how HU enhances her work with animals.

When Oi and I took a three-day mini vacation to celebrate our anniversary, a neighbor attended to our cats' needs conscientiously. However, when we returned, JJ and Peaches were visibly upset that we had left them alone and let us know by their standoffish behavior. Other pet owners have reported similar experiences. Sharon offered a solution which evolved from a question she had asked the Inner Teacher: "How can I use divine creativity with the HU and the animals?"

Surprisingly, she was told by the Inner Teacher to invite pets whose owners had left town, either on vacation or for business, to a morning HU. This invitation is also extended to animals with behavioral challenges. Roll is never taken during the morning HU, where the animals play, socialize, and connect with Divine Spirit.

Sharon always asks permission from the owners before working with their pets. She informs the animals how many "lights and darks" their "parents" will be gone, who will be caring for them, and whether they will be staying with them or coming and going; if the latter, how often? Pets want to be assured that the person attending to them knows about food, treats, play time, and walks. Sharon answers all of their questions and tells the animals about the love song of HU. They especially enjoy meeting with other animals in the morning HU each day when their parents are gone.

Parents report coming home to happy and welcoming pets. Sharon suggested another option—play the HU Song for your animals while you're away. This dovetails with her second tip involving lost animals.

Sharon related the story of a family who was moving to another state. Once they had arrived at their destination and were unloading, one of their two cats escaped from its carrier and disappeared from view. The owners called Sharon in a panic.

She instructed them to place a recording of HU in the area where they had last seen their pet along with its litter box and a toy. At the same time, Sharon reached out inwardly and asked the cat's Higher Self to listen for the sound of HU, then follow it back to safety. Within an hour, the cat emerged from the darkness and was reunited with the family.

We were curious to know how Sharon presents the idea of inviting pets to a morning HU to their owners. She explained that she asks them if they would be willing to try a spiritual exercise which could help their pets while they are gone. Some owners are interested in learning more during their conversation, while others agree without questioning her further.

When these owners return to happy, calm, well-behaved pets, they ask Sharon to tell them about the morning HU.

She usually recommends a video called, "HU: Experience the Sound of Soul." In this popular YouTube clip, the benefits of singing *HU* are enumerated in concert with the song.[2]

*   *   *

While my judgment about quinoa salad from Chapter Seven was mildly limiting in nature, I can think of other judgments that are especially debilitating. One in particular comes to mind: "If I open my heart to love again, my heart will be broken." I now use a variety of spiritual exercises to address such judgments as well as fears bubbling up from my past. Of course, some wounds take longer to heal than others even with the support of the Inner Teacher and the best of tools.

At age thirty-five, when my mom translated from this life, I had little understanding of how to cope with such a grievous loss. A memorable experience in Mexico a few months later proved to be a turning point in my healing. It brought me closer to the Inner Teacher and helped ease the pain of losing my mom.

The Dogs of Puerto Vallarta

A two-thousand-dollar settlement from my seventh car accident enabled me to buy a ticket to Mexico where I planned to live for the winter and heal my broken heart. I had no idea how long I could live on the small bundle of traveler's checks I carried with me in my wallet, but I set sail on this new adventure despite the inconvenience of a lonely headwind.

One and a half months—that's how long two thousand dollars lasted in the tourist town of Puerto Vallarta in 1985. My first choice had been Cancun; however, my plans abruptly changed when a hurricane swept through that coastal town not long before my departure date.

I survived on my meager savings and a few key Spanish words that I remembered from high school. This allowed me to rent a room at a small hotel on the outskirts of town and order food at a nearby restaurant. Since I had given up alcohol by this time in my life and wasn't interested in socializing, I kept to myself. By some cosmic coincidence, a realtor I knew from southern Oregon decided to move to Puerto Vallarta to sell time shares at Mismaloya Beach where the famous movie, "Night of the Iguana," was filmed. We met occasionally for dinner, but I spent most of my time alone on the beach and writing in my journal.

Sunsets are beautiful in Puerto Vallarta. Often I would remain on the beach until well after dark. I would contemplate, think about my mom, and speak inwardly to the Inner Teacher as best I could. During this time, I learned to appreciate this connection more and more. I found comfort in the fact that I was not completely alone in life. One evening, the Inner Teacher sent an unexpected gift.

It was just after dark, and the beach was nearly deserted. A couple of stray dogs were lingering about, but almost no tourists. Seeing the many homeless animals in the tourist town tugged at my heart. I sang *HU* for a good half hour with my eyes closed while lying on my back on a worn hotel blanket. As I was falling asleep, I felt something brush lightly up against my right leg. I opened one eye and discovered that a dog had snuggled up next to my body! To my astonishment, another dog took his place on my left side.

I continued singing *HU* and fell asleep appreciating the companionship and love of these two animals. Then, the Inner Teacher sent even more love. When I awoke, I found two more dogs pressed up against my upper body on each side. The five of us basked in the love of HU a good portion of the evening.

I remember Puerto Vallarta with fond memories. None are more special than "the night of the four stray dogs." Their love helped heal my heart. I hope their lives are better for the song of HU and the appreciation of a passing stranger.

As I checked in my suitcases the morning I was leaving for Oregon, I looked in my wallet. I had exactly ten dollars and a dime in change. When the airline clerk informed me that a new airport fee had recently gone into effect for all outgoing flights, my heart sank.

"That will be ten dollars," the lady announced. So, I flew home with ten cents in my pocket and some colorful stories to share with friends. My trip to Mexico was money well spent for a healing of the heart.

HU Praja and the Golden Globe by Pichaya

Beagles typically howl, but HU Praja sings. His owner, Dio McMahon, once told me that her Beagle sings *HU* when he is asleep. She named him after the spiritual teacher, Prajapati. Learning about a Beagle singing *HU* fascinated me. I wished to hear him sing for me one day.

A few months after Dio's husband, Kevin, made a peaceful transition, Dio asked me to stay at her house and take care of her dog while she would be away from home for ten days. I was happy to be there for Dio and eager to spend time with HU Praja.

The first day, HU Praja and I walked for a few hours in the woods. During our five-mile hike, he would stop and sniff anything he found interesting along the path. When he detected a specific scent, he would announce his new discovery excitedly and loudly to the whole forest with his deep howl.

While I was anxious to continue our walk, HU Praja would take his time. He focused intently on his hunting game, his nose glued to the ground. Every few steps, he would stop, sniff, and howl. For him, the joy was in the journey. Observing his behavior, I realized that he was teaching me to be more patient. Walking with HU Praja was a reminder to stop, smell the roses, and enjoy the little things in life such as the natural beauty around me. When HU Praja howled, I could join him with the love song of HU.

We retired for the night after our adventuresome hike and an early dinner. He insisted on being close and crawled up beside me on the bed. With a pleading expression in his sweet brown eyes, my heart melted. It was the first time in my entire life that I had allowed a dog to sleep next to me.

Early the next morning, I was awakened by HU Praja's snoring. I then heard the sound of HU and wondered where it was originating. When I opened my eyes, to my surprise, I saw HU Praja sitting up in bed with his head tilted back singing *HU*. Witnessing this miracle made my heart dance. Yet, there was more.

After patting him on the head and thanking him for singing *HU*, I turned to my left and checked the time on the clock. It was precisely 4:00 a.m. To my astonishment, I saw a golden globe floating in the air a few inches away. An immense wave of warm love radiated from the illuminated sphere of light.

I recognized the loving energy and instantly knew that it was Kevin visiting me in his Soul body. At that moment, I remembered what he had shared with me the day before he translated. I had asked him what wisdom he would like to pass along to the next generation. "Be true to yourself," he replied.

Seeing him cloaked in his glowing globe of beautiful golden light took my breath away. Intuitively, I knew that he was happy and free. Evidently, HU Praja had seen Kevin appear in his Soul body earlier and greeted him by singing *HU*.

The next night, I had a vivid dream. Kevin was joyfully playing a violin in the family room, smiling and swaying happily from side to side. Gazing over at me with his hazel eyes, Kevin told me, "I wrote this love song for Dio."

My memorable week with HU Praja was filled with many miracles. I am grateful for the gift of witnessing a Beagle singing *HU*. Seeing Kevin in his Soul body and meeting him in my dream were powerful confirmations that love will never die. The song of HU connected the three of us that morning with divine love which transcends space and time.

The Goats of HU by Pichaya

Animals love the song of HU. They are drawn to the celestial music like a magnet. My trips to a farm with Mike have proven this to be true.

When Mike was drinking raw goat milk, we would purchase it from a very kind man named Dennis. His goats loved him. Every time Dennis was out of their sight, they would call for him and scream loudly like children throwing a tantrum. It was painful to hear the crying goats. Mike and I did our best to console them by singing *HU*.

One day, while Mike was engaged in a lively discussion with Dennis inside the barn, I was waiting outside by the fence watching the tribe of goats standing fifty feet away enjoying their breakfast. They looked peaceful and content chewing the fresh green grass. They appeared to live in the moment, not thinking about the past or worrying about the future. They were demonstrating what it means to just be.

Observing the goats, I realized how much God loves us. I felt happy to be alive, to love and be loved. I appreciated Dennis for his wonderful service to our community. I also appreciated all life around me: the friendly black dog, the adventuresome cat, the lush green grass beneath tall Fir and Pine, and puffy white clouds in the deep blue sky. My heart was filled with boundless love. As this love overflowed, I felt inspired to sing *HU* and tell God, "I love you."

The moment I sang *HU*, one goat suddenly stopped chewing grass, turned her head, and made eye contact with me. The doe began to walk confidently in my direction. She stopped a few steps away and stared up at me with a sweet look in her eyes as if to say, "Please serenade me with *HU*." A few seconds later, the rest of the herd followed the leader.

Soon, eight of them lined up joyfully, side by side, gazing at me with a mellow and affectionate look in their eyes while I continued singing *HU*. Clearly, they were drawn to the powerful energy of this sacred song and immense love that flowed through me. Before we left, I took pictures of these wonderful Souls who willingly posed for a group portrait to commemorate their first time hearing the song of HU.

- 11 -

SHARING THE GIFT OF HU

"Anytime is a good time to share the HU song with anyone in a trying situation."

—Harold Klemp
*A Modern Prophet Answers
Your Key Questions about Life,
Book 3*[1]

I had only heard about the Sound Current of HU a few weeks prior to loaning a book called *ECKANKAR—The Key to Secret Worlds* to a co-worker at the plywood mill where I was employed in my twenties. Admittedly, I was still unsure what the teaching was all about. *Was there any truth to what Paul Twitchell had written in his book?* I wondered. I was searching for confirmation.

What Would Bob Think?

I remember the apprehension I felt when I demonstrated to Bob how to sing the sacred word, HU. What would he think about HU and, equally important, what would he think about me after reading the aforementioned book?

When I saw Bob shortly thereafter, he thanked me for sharing the book with him. He was happy with his current beliefs but had found the spiritual exercises and singing *HU* "interesting." Bob had achieved immediate success, but upon hearing his story, I realized that I should have taken more time in explaining the various sounds he could hear during contemplation. Up until this point, my spiritual exercises had yielded only a modicum of inner peace.

Bob, however, had seen flashes of lightening and heard distant claps of thunder when he had closed his eyes. He related how he had gone to the window only to find a sky filled with stars. His first contemplation had been a huge success, I reassured him. Thunder and lightening were reportedly sounds of the Audible Life Stream associated with the physical plane. But the tone in his voice conveyed that he had found this experience quite overwhelming. Surprisingly, when I left my job at the plywood mill for a return to college, Bob told me that he still sang *HU* as part of his prayers.

Listening to Bob share his inner experience inspired me to continue with my daily contemplations. I later realized the Inner Teacher had used my co-worker to verify the reality of the Sound Current of HU at this important juncture in my life.

As a result, I resolved to be more thoughtful and thorough in my initial explanations of both the sound of HU and the Inner Teacher. This interaction with Bob influenced my decision to share HU mainly through my writing where I could provide more groundwork for those willing to examine something new.

"That Wonderful Word"

When we write from experience, our words carry a vibration which can resonate deeply with a reader. Some call this "writing from the heart." Consequently, I have always been a proponent of sharing with others what has helped me. HU falls into this category.

One afternoon, out of the blue, I received a call from a woman in the Midwest who had read about the significance of HU and the benefits derived from singing the sacred word with love. While I don't recall the woman's name or in what context she had read what I'd written, I do remember the excitement in her voice as she thanked me for sharing "that wonderful word."

She had suffered with back pain for many years and, according to her, had exhausted all avenues for resolving the issue. But now, after singing *HU* for several weeks and visualizing a golden stream of love vibrating up and down her spine, she was finally enjoying relief. For a writer, receiving a call like this is the highest honor and greatest possible reward.

Two Silent Spiritual Teachers by Pichaya

Throughout my life, family, friends, and strangers have been drawn to me for advice. Often I simply listen, but when an opportunity arises, I share the gift of HU with those who are open to receive it. A conversation with my sister in Thailand on a video call was a life-changing experience for both of us.

In the year 2005, Noot was diagnosed with an ovarian tumor during her early stages of pregnancy. Although it was benign, she was concerned that it might spread and potentially endanger the fetus. Feeling frightened by this disturbing news, she asked me what to do.

In Thai culture, the eldest sister in the family receives a high level of respect, and I have earned the trust of my three younger sisters. When asked for advice, I always encourage them to go within and listen for their inner guidance; however, on this certain day, Noot was more interested in knowing how I had overcome my fear when I was confronted with a similar situation.

Following my inner nudge, I asked her, "Are you open to learning something new?"

With tears in her eyes, she replied, "I am willing to try anything."

I continued, "There is a love song called HU. It is an ancient name for God. When I sing this sacred word, I experience miracles. It brings peace in times of trouble. It helps me overcome fear and protects me from harm. It opens my heart to receive more of God's love."

Fascinated by the benefits of singing *HU* as I described them, Noot's eyes lit up. "Please teach me how to sing that love song," she requested.

With specific instructions, I spoke calmly, "Find a quiet place and time to be alone. Sit comfortably, take a few deep breaths, and close your eyes. Put your attention on your third eye. Then, sing *HU* for up to twenty minutes and listen for inner guidance. Do this every day. Open your heart to receive all the love that is coming your way." Then, I demonstrated how to sing *HU*.

The sweet song of HU affected Noot so profoundly that it inspired her to join in. As a Buddhist, she is familiar with meditation where one sits in silence after chanting an entire book of Pali scripture. With the song of HU, she was happy and eager to sing only one sacred word.

In the days that followed, Noot shared with me her inner experience of singing *HU*. She had seen a blue light and heard the soothing sound of a waterfall during contemplation. Furthermore, a tall man with a white beard and a beautiful woman in a blue dress had appeared on her inner screen multiple times, standing in silence and smiling at her. Their presence brought a sense of peace, love, and calmness that she had not felt in several months.

With curiosity, Noot questioned me about these mysterious individuals. I sent her the group portrait of several spiritual teachers and asked if she could identify any of them. As soon as she received my message, Noot requested a video call. The moment we connected, Noot exclaimed, "You won't believe this." Her eyes widened as she pointed to the pictures of Rami Nuri and Kata Daki.[2] "These are the people who appeared in my contemplation."

Sharing the golden gift of HU with Noot brought us closer than we had ever been before. A few months later, she informed me that her pain had miraculously subsided, and the tumor had disappeared completely. Noot successfully delivered a healthy baby without any complications. Not only did my sister meet those wonderful spiritual teachers who had given her hope, opened her heart, and showered her with love, Noot was also healed by the power of HU.

Cindy "Who?" by Pichaya

When my children were attending elementary school, I met a beautiful Chinese woman at the bus stop in front of our house. She was the nanny of my neighbor's children, who were the same ages as my two younger ones. Every day, we smiled at each other because Cindy did not speak much English, only "hello" and "goodbye." Fortunately, she carried an electronic translator in her jacket and relied on the children to communicate for her.

I was going through chronic depression at the time and still coping with my health challenges; hence, I was not as friendly as I naturally would have been.

I did not feel like socializing with anyone, including Cindy. My heart was closed.

One night, while I was feeling down and thinking negatively about myself, the Inner Teacher suggested, "Why don't you make friends with Cindy?"

I asked, "How?"

"You can teach her English," was the reply.

Consequently, I invited Cindy to join me for a cup of tea the very next day. When asked if she would be interested in learning how to speak English, she typed the word "Yes" into the translator.

Cindy became an excellent student. Her assignment involved writing about her daily activities, including new ideas or insights about life. Over time, her English gradually improved, and our friendship grew.

One day, Cindy confided in me about her personal life challenges. I listened attentively. She then asked, "What should I do?"

After consulting with the Inner Teacher inwardly, I shared the gift of HU with Cindy and encouraged her to write down her inner experiences in a journal. The following week, she approached me with a happy smile. Cindy reported that she had heard the sound of a flute and had seen a white light on her inner screen. She felt more at ease and, subsequently, her troubling situation resolved itself.

Cindy and I have been close friends ever since. When I give without expectation and serve life with love, I receive more love in return. In this case, I was given a lasting friendship worth more than gold. Surprisingly, I learned later that Cindy's last name is "HU."

A New Form of Prayer by Pichaya

An unforgettable experience on New Year's Eve in 2011 taught me a valuable lesson about the importance of carefully following the Inner Teacher's guidance. After I kissed my children goodnight, I read a few passages in a book about love and retired for the night. I tossed and turned. Feeling restless, I was unable to sleep until suddenly, at midnight, a strong inner nudge prompted me to check my Facebook page. There was only one message, an urgent request from a friend in Jordon asking me to respond as soon as possible.

Jouri was confronted with a serious personal crisis. She described in detail how she had contemplated several different ways to take her own life. I contacted her immediately and asked if she would like to meet on Skype even though it was 1:00 a.m. in Oregon.

When we connected, I could tell by her eyes that she had been crying for many hours. She told me that her life was not working. Her relationship, health, career, and finances were collapsing all at once. There was no point in living anymore. I listened with compassion as she poured out her heart.

She asked, "Can you help me?"

I replied, "I am happy to help you in any way I can."

Jouri informed me that she had studied her Bible, but God had not answered her prayers. She felt forsaken. "I need a prayer," she pleaded.

"Would you be interested in a new form of prayer?" I asked her.

"Anything," she replied.

I introduced her to the song of HU. As she sang along with me, she felt an immediate shift in her consciousness. She told me that a wave of warm love had enveloped her entire body, and the heaviness in her heart was lifted. At that moment, for the first time in several months of despair, she felt at peace. Wiping her tears, she added, "You have saved my life. I want to live."

"In times of trouble, please remember to sing *HU*," I reminded her. "It will continue to heal your heart and allow you to view your challenges from a higher perspective."

There is no greater joy than making a difference in someone's life. Jouri and I were brought together by the Inner Teacher, two Facebook friends living on opposite sides of the world, to share the love and support we receive from singing *HU*. It is a gift from the Inner Teacher that opens everyone's heart regardless of race, religion, or distance between them. This beautiful love song even touches the hearts of animals.

"I Love You, Anami" by Pichaya

Anami was a family dog who loved the song of HU. Each morning during my contemplation, she would sit next to me with her ears perked up, tongue hanging out, and eyes shining brightly. She would wait patiently for me to finish singing *HU* and take her out for a ride followed by a walk in the woods. Anami was a happy, fluffy, loving Keeshond, who was my constant companion. She was my shadow.

The kitchen was Anami's favorite place. While I prepared meals, she would sit by my side waiting for something interesting to be dropped. Her ears perked up when she heard me chopping vegetables and meat. She even enjoyed carrots, celery, and bits of broccoli that would accidentally fall to the floor. She knew I couldn't resist giving her a piece of raw chicken or rib eye steak when she looked up at me with her sweet and adoring eyes.

One of her greatest thrills was going for a ride. She would sit on the passenger seat, her head sticking out the window. With her mouth fully open and tongue hanging out, her jowls would flap loosely in the breeze. Her thick fur coat danced joyfully with the wind. She would squeal gleefully as if to exclaim, "Life is good."

As the years passed by, Anami became extremely ill; yet, she was still eager to please me. When I was feeling blue, she would do anything to bring me joy. She knew exactly how to make me smile. She would roll over multiple times without me asking even when her body was in pain. Then, she would cover her eyes with her paws—acting shy—just to brighten up my day.

Knowing that she would be free from unnecessary suffering, we made arrangements with an in-home pet euthanasia service to assist with Anami's transition. Even though we had prepared for this heart-wrenching process several weeks in advance, it was still exceedingly difficult for us to accept the fact that the day had finally arrived. In contrast, for Anami, all was well in her world because she lived only in the moment. She was simply happy to be with us.

Anami's ears perked up when she heard the familiar jingle of my car keys early in the evening of our appointment. Enthusiastically, she raced to the door leading to the garage, gazing at me with her dark brown eyes that said, "Let's go for a ride." I wept uncontrollably as I drove her around town one last time.

There were many tears as our family formed a circle on the kitchen floor. We offered her treats as she walked up to each family member. She licked our hands and plopped her body down in front of me. Sobbing, I told her, "I love you, Anami."

I sang *HU* the entire time, even after the vet gave her the injection. Surrounded by her loving family, with her chin resting in my left palm, Anami looked at me intently one more time before taking her last breath and closing her eyes forever.

The vet commented on how special the ceremony had been and asked, "What were you saying?"

"I was singing Anami's favorite song, the song of HU," I answered. Then, she asked what it meant.

"It is a love song that brings peace, joy, and love in times of need."

The woman smiled and thanked me for sharing this beautiful song of HU.

- 12 -
LOVE IS A NEVER-ENDING STORY

"Wherever you are, and whatever you do, be in love."

—Rumi[1]

Since learning how the Inner Teacher's role complements that of the Voice of HU, I've come to view them as fairly synonymous. When I'm singing *HU*, for example, I feel the love of the Inner Teacher; when I hear the Voice of HU, I sometimes see the face of the Inner Teacher smiling back at me on my inner screen.

I wrote the preceding paragraph at the beginning of Chapter Two, but it felt out of place. As I've mentioned previously, everything has its place in my life, including words. Now I know why. That lead paragraph was always meant to be here. I'm a little embarrassed to admit it, but only this morning did I realize who the Inner Teacher really is.

The Inner Teacher is the Voice of HU—the highest aspect of the Creator—incarnating in its universe as itself. The Inner Teacher is the Living Word made flesh.

The True Purpose of the Inner Teacher

While driving along the North Umpqua Highway toward Crater Lake in Oregon one day, I considered different ways in which I could introduce the song of HU and the Inner Teacher. I'd been invited to be the emcee for a small local gathering where the public would be welcome.

As I was enjoying the unobstructed view of the river and exploring possible scenarios, I heard these words forming softly in my mind: "Would you like to know the true purpose of the Inner Teacher?"

I quickly pulled into the driveway of someone's farmhouse and reached for my pen. Yes, of course I wanted to hear more. The answer I anticipated was "to lead Soul home to God." If asked today, however, I would respond differently. Since then, I've arrived at a paramount realization: Life is all about love. Here is what I was told:

The true purpose of the Inner Teacher is to shower us with love until we realize that nothing else exists.

Thankfully, I have experienced this love firsthand on more than one occasion. I have absolute certainty about the love and support of the Inner Teacher for those under his care. Although this endless love of the Teacher is given *carte blanche*, in my case, awareness of this gift heightened when I began moving beyond my comfort zone, albeit a baby step at a time. Then, one day, I found myself metaphorically standing at the edge of the world.

Up until then, one daunting fear had stalked me from the shadows on my journey through life. Suddenly, it was out in the open, directly in front of me, blocking my path. A confrontation was inevitable. It was clear that I could go no further without facing this terrifying beast—the Black Jaguar on steroids. It was the fear of public speaking.

Chicago

At no time in my life did I appreciate the love and support of the Inner Teacher more than when I faced "The Crisis in Chicago." Without question, my battle with the fear of public speaking could rival "The Thrilla in Manilla" in which Ali had defeated Joe Frazier in 1975 using the now legendary rope-a-dope tactic. During my memorable battle with this fear, when *The Secret Language of Waking Dreams* was published by Eckankar in 1992, I'd been asked to speak at several small gatherings. I had come out on top, but like Ali, there would be other brutal fights ahead.

One such rematch happened in Chicago where I was scheduled to speak at a large seminar at 7:00 p.m. on Saturday night, not long before Sri Harold Klemp, the spiritual leader of Eckankar, who was the featured speaker. As per my usual routine, I sequestered myself in my room and monitored my thoughts to ensure that no negativity intruded upon my well-rehearsed fifteen-minute talk.

Around 5:00, I decided to practice my presentation one last time. To my surprise and horror, I couldn't remember a single word. Panic doesn't come close to describing what I was feeling, but it was definitely the lead car in a long train of frightening emotions.

After a few moments, I was able to settle down enough to ask inwardly for help. I repeated these impassioned words aloud: "Inner Teacher, I'm here for you; now I'm asking you to be here for me."

Within thirty seconds, the most delicate wave of serenity and love flooded my entire being. I didn't want to move. I wanted to feel that way forever. When my alarm went off twenty minutes later, I took the elevator downstairs, checked in at the backstage desk, and calmly took a seat to await my turn to go on stage.

I was so relaxed that I hardly heard my name being called. Fifteen minutes flew by. I heard the words I'd practiced flowing smoothly from my lips, but they sounded distant and surreal. Still wrapped in a blanket of the Inner Teacher's love, I wondered if I had not been taken to the Soul Plane.

I experienced the Inner Teacher's boundless love that night and know that each person who is willing to take a risk will find the same love and level of support that I enjoyed. Oi has experienced this, too. During a tumultuous period of her life, the Inner Teacher was there to honor an ancient promise.

"I Am Always with You" by Pichaya

The Inner Teacher sent a powerful message in an unexpected way to answer an important question in 2001 during a major crisis. I lived in a small apartment in Albuquerque, New Mexico, with my first husband, James, who introduced me to the Inner Teacher. We had two small children, a two-year-old boy named Nate and a nine-month-old baby girl, Jamie. A few months before, we had discovered that he was terminally ill and would soon make his transition.

We had recently moved back from Thailand and were adjusting to our new season of life. During this time, we were living on food stamps with very limited resources. Each day, I helplessly watched James' health decline and denied the fact that one day he would leave me.

One night, James shared an inner experience where he met his departed loved ones. "My mom and dad are waiting for me on the other side," he told me.

James looked me in the eyes and whispered softly, "Please take good care of yourself and our children. I love you."

Hearing those words, I realized that James would finally leave the physical body forever. My heart shattered as I broke down in tears. Sobbing uncontrollably, I did not know what to do.

Then, I remembered to sing *HU* and asked my Teacher in contemplation, "How am I going to survive in this country and raise my children alone?" In that sacred moment, I felt the warm presence of the Inner Teacher envelope me as I continued to sing *HU*.

Suddenly, Jamie started crying in her bedroom. For some unknown reason, I turned on the radio when I entered the room. While picking her up, I heard the announcer say, "Everything will be alright. I am always with you."

That same evening, a friend of ours named Amy arrived from San Francisco to offer emotional support and help with my children during this transition. The very next morning, James translated. Amy contacted a hospice nurse, a social worker, and a close friend of mine. Within twenty minutes, all of them arrived at my door. I thought I would be completely alone, but God sent these wonderful people to help me through this crisis. My heart overflowed with love and gratitude.

The Inner Teacher continued to shower me with the miracles of love. A friendly man delivered a large box filled with cheese, crackers, and dried food. He said in a comforting voice, "Your friend, Diane, from California called our church about your loss. We are sorry. Here is food for you and your children." Thai monks also brought us delicious Thai food and desserts while friends donated clothes for my children and me.

Singing *HU* was an open door to a higher state of awareness. I realized that the radio announcement was a timely message sent to comfort me in my time of need. The statement, "I am always with you," is a promise from the Inner Teacher, reassuring me that I will always be loved and supported throughout dark times.

* * *

The Universe *IS* Love

The universe was created by HU and is presently sustained by Its vibrant life force. The consciousness of HU embodies the entire universe. In fact, the universe *is* HU. Since the Creator is love, we can know that, at its deepest level, the universe is also love. HU can be heard in the sound of the rain, the laughter of children, the whistle of the locomotive, the chirping of birds, as well as deep in caves as the sound of silence. Indeed, everything is HU.

Beethoven

For a brief time in my twenties, I listened to classical music. My favorite was Beethoven's Ninth Symphony. One morning, after a long night's work at the local plywood mill, I leaned back in my easy chair. My body was tired, and my eyes were heavy. Beethoven's symphony was playing on my stereo in the background. I was about to fall asleep, when suddenly I heard his composition as I'd never heard it before.

Music was not only coming from my speakers, it was emanating from the four walls of the room and ceiling. It was the most uplifting and inexplicable experience I could have ever imagined. Words fail when describing such a moment.

This was really the Symphony of HU serenading me with love and joy, with Beethoven's help of course. It's no wonder the fourth and final movement of his Ninth Symphony is called "Ode to Joy." It was a divine moment of ecstasy. The Inner Teacher would grant me another glimpse into the inner workings of the Universe, and my relationship to it, but I would have to wait three decades for the experience.

Everything Is Light and Sound

One sunny afternoon, I was driving through the Oregon countryside enjoying a clear view of Mt. Hood with its snow-laden summit. Without forewarning or intention, I suddenly found myself in an altered state of consciousness. One minute I was the driver of a swiftly moving vehicle enjoying the greenery of spring, the next I was conscious of everything in my universe!

There was nothing that was not made from the Light and Sound of God. I gazed out in awe upon the fields and pastures I had driven past countless times. There were cows and horses, fences and barns. They were only Light. And the roadway with its approaching cars, also Divine Light. Above me soared sparrows and hawks, blackbirds, and doves. The wind that carried them and the mountain that inspired them vibrated with the love of Spirit. All things big and small were clothed in the Light and Sound of God.

My consciousness touched all that surrounded me. For several minutes I was no-thing, yet everything. My driving was not affected; a part of me was left in charge of the mundane.

With this realization came only knowingness. It was stark, still, unassuming, colorless, odorless. There was joy, but not the joy of having or doing. It was the sheer joy of pure beingness. It was calm, peaceful, serene, and free. Perhaps this realization would have been more profound accompanied by flutes and violins, I do not know. The silence was remarkable in its own right. I had experienced ecstasy while listening to Beethoven, but this was surprisingly different; it simply *was*.

Shortly after I had recognized the common thread of Light and Sound in everything around me, it struck me that living in the present moment did indeed make me happy, at least *that* present moment. Others were best left forgotten in my opinion. Thus, I found it peculiar to remember a rather grueling high school math class while reflecting upon my recent esoteric experience. Perhaps those who excelled in math will appreciate how I used Geometry to determine that I am HU.

If A = B and B = C, then A must also = C

I always remembered this axiom called "the transitive property of equality" from high school Geometry. Math wasn't my favorite subject, but I could hold my own with something like a B minus average. English I could handle with one arm tied behind my back.

Instead of pursuing higher math, I traded my Calculus book for a study hall pass. Rather than going to the library each day, I left school through a back door and walked to the small lunch cafe my brother owned a stone's throw away from the school. The Andy Griffith Show aired at 11:30 a.m. in those days and watching TV made me happier than sitting in the library looking up at the clock. In a way, one episode of the Andy Griffith Show mirrored my own life.

Buddy Ebsen made a guest appearance in the role of a drifter, whom Andy hired to paint the fence in front of their house. Buddy's character came up with any number of excuses to avoid the work. One day, he talked Opie, Andy's son, into skipping school and going fishing with him.

When Opie asked Buddy why he was going fishing when there was work to be done, Buddy told Opie his secret of happiness. He replied (paraphrased), "It's a man's duty to make himself happy, to live in the moment. That fence can wait until tomorrow. You see, tomorrow is the greatest day ever invented. You can do anything tomorrow. Today the fish are calling."

Finally, Andy had to fire Buddy, not only because he didn't follow through with painting the fence, but more so because Opie began imitating Buddy's actions. When Opie was asked to take out the garbage, he told his father that he would do it tomorrow because tomorrow was the best day every invented. In a way, Buddy exerted an influence on me, too.

"I will go to the library and study tomorrow," I told myself. But somehow, I seldom followed through. On the positive side, I learned a little bit about being happy in the present moment.

I can't say that I've changed my view of math since high school, but I can appreciate one thing about it. In a roundabout way, it taught me that I must be HU. Here is the tried and true axiom once again, and how I was finally able to put it to good use in a spiritual application.

If $A = B$ and $B = C$, then A must also $= C$

If I am the universe and the universe is HU, then I must also be HU.

* * *

Love Is a Never-ending Story

As Oi and I were finishing our final draft, I expressed my deep appreciation to the Inner Teacher for the many insights we'd been given while writing about the various facets of HU. It never occurred to me at the outset that I'd gain a greater understanding of the Law of Silence during this process or cultivate a closer relationship with the Inner Teacher. Writing a story about my father and the pain I felt upon losing my mom was also unexpected.

The preeminent revelation, without question, was the existence of The Golden Book. It opened a door that will surely lead to further insights on my continuing journey as Soul. While reclining in our living room wondering what the future might hold, I heard the distinctive Voice from the Sanctuary:

"Your life is but a chapter in a never-ending story. You are love itself, infinite and eternal. Your dramas, your discoveries, your lessons and adventures, are memorialized forever within the pages of The Golden Book of HU. From your first steps forth from the Ocean of Love, you have created dreams and have lived them to the fullest. As a Universal Traveler, you have left your footprints on countless worlds including this one where an aspect of your Greater Being has chosen to visit.

"As a drop from the Infinite Ocean of Love, you wield unlimited power, for love is unlimited power, and that is what you are. Be wary of those who say you are less. You are an emissary of the Divine, imbued with creative imagination, choosing to dream that you have stepped away from Infinity, if only for a moment, to smell a rose, to paddle a canoe, to climb a mountain, to hug a child. Every dream inspired by love endures. The rest are swept away like the leaves in Autumn.

"In your world, love makes the rivers sing and the wild apples shine. Love feeds the flowers and lifts multi-colored birds into azure skies. Yet, how many feel this sustaining presence without knowing its source? When you discover love at the core of your being, you cannot help but express that love in creative ways that bring joy and satisfaction. As a co-creator with the Ocean of Love, there is nothing beyond your ability, not even the creation of worlds.

"Do not doubt that you are fully supported by my love in every way. Your greatest service is to accept my love with a generous heart and let it pour out and uplift those around you, those struggling, those crying for love, those who feel unworthy to receive it. Listen for the voice of the Inner Teacher when you are in anguish; listen for it when you are dancing with the wind; listen for it when you are holding your beloved; when you are turning back the covers on your bed at night.

"The consciousness of the Voice of HU flows through this Sanctuary from above on its way to my myriad creations in the worlds of polarity. When you stood within the energy field in the Wings of the Wind house in Sedona,[2] you were connected with my Voice which infuses all with love, healing, wisdom, or whatever a wanting Soul needs. Nothing is held back, as long as it is in alignment with divine love and Soul's own self-imposed rules and limitations that it has adopted in order to learn a lesson or better understand my creation.

"All Souls are envoys of their Unlimited Selves. They have taken on limitation in order to learn, to love, or simply to pursue adventure. There are those who come to study the mechanics of polarity, then incorporate what they have learned into their own creations. You'll notice that some whom you may encounter here in the Atma Lok, *the Soul Plane, have not yet traveled to the lower regions of coarse vibrations.*

"The most courageous Souls accept the daunting challenge of experiencing every possibility imaginable in the worlds of duality. Why would any Soul choose hardship and pain? To expand its capacity to love. In this universe, and the majority of others, this is the motivating principle. The common thread running through them all is the Inner Teacher, the Ultimate Emissary of Love.

"When the pages of The Golden Book are filled, it will be sealed. It will then be enshrined with treasures from other universes in a sacred location within the Infinite Ocean of Love. I know that your mind is struggling to understand how this would be possible. Let it go for now.

"Thank you for participating in this project which is, for you and Oi, a labor of love. And thank you for visiting my house on your adventuresome journey. It is my humble honor to serve as your host. Now, be at peace."

The Voice of HU fell silent. I felt enveloped by the love of the Creator as I gradually became aware of my physical surroundings. The rattling of pots and pans in the kitchen told me Oi was preparing dinner. I offered to help, knowing she would find this amusing. She smiled. I could see that she had placed the garbage can at the edge of the kitchen. *Was this really an appropriate task for a potential creator of worlds?* I mused, chuckling to myself.

Then, as I ventured forth in the direction of the trash bin on my mission for the misses, I heard the Voice of HU within the recesses of my heart:

"Remember, Beloved, your life is but a chapter in a never-ending story. You are love itself, infinite and eternal."

Epilogue:
The Sound of Spiritual Freedom

*"When you get a little more spiritual freedom,
love comes into your heart and replaces fear with wisdom. This is the golden heart."*

—Harold Klemp
The Call of Soul[1]

Upon completing this book, I thanked the Inner Teacher for traveling with us on our memorable journey. While I had resisted the urge to tilt at windmills along the way, I did pull over once or twice to sample the local cuisine. Of course, nothing tastes better than good old home cooking with extra large helpings of divine love and spiritual freedom.

Ironically, midway through our journey, instead of going faster, I found myself driving slower and slower until we finally arrived at our destination—the present moment.

I made a request of the Inner Teacher: "Please remind me what it feels like to be totally free." I wasn't expecting a profound experience; perhaps a feeling of peace or a day free of worry.

I received my answer as I was falling asleep one evening. As Oi and I were stepping into a hot air balloon in a dreamlike setting, I heard these words from the Inner Teacher:

"I love you unconditionally. Once you allow yourself to receive my love without conditions, you will find inner peace and total alignment with the Divine. This will enable you to rise above outer concerns."

A Festival of Balloons was happening around us, not unlike such galas held back on earth. But I had the inner knowingness that we were lifting off from a position within the temple grounds. I was holding Oi's hand, marveling at the picturesque scene below—gardens of exotic flowers, wildlife, ponds lined with Willows, the reflection from the golden Sanctuary dome, the coming and going of Souls, colorful globes of light resembling the balloons decorating the air around us.

There was also a feeling of satisfaction in the air and a sense that a mission, perhaps even a journey, had been completed. I looked deeply into the Inner Teacher's eyes and silently expressed my gratitude for his love and service to all life. I had grown to appreciate this great being's role even more after realizing his true identity as the highest aspect of the Creator.

As we climbed higher, I noticed that the air was staying consistently the same temperature. I'm sure Oi also noticed how quiet and still our ascent had become. We reveled in pure and peaceful silence. Then, Oi and I looked at each other quizzically. We both became aware of it at the same time. We heard the barely audible sound of a flute behind the curtain of silence. It was coming from the Sanctuary, now far below us. We glanced over at the Inner Teacher to see if he had noticed it, too.

"Dear ones," he said turning to face us, "if you listen closely, you'll detect yet another sound behind the single note of the flute. It is the sound of *HU*; more accurately, it is the Voice of HU within the heart of the Sanctuary. It is the sound all Souls yearn to hear. It is the sound of spiritual freedom."

Acknowledgments

Special thanks to Karla Joy McMechan who offered her loving support in addition to completing our initial edit. We would also like to thank Sharon Sheppard for giving us a glimpse into the role HU plays in her mission as an animal communicator. Sharon's contact information appears in the Notes section of this book under Acknowledgments.[1]

Our heartfelt appreciation goes out Claude Gruffy for helping us with our graphics and Rose Elphick,[3] our typesetter, for her kindness and patience during the final phase of polishing this book.

Notes

Preface

1) Please see *ECKOPEDIA: The ECKANKAR Lexicon,* by Harold Klemp (Eckankar, 2023), page 294, for a definition of "Temple of Golden Wisdom."
2) Harold Klemp, "HU: A Love Song to God," CD (Eckankar, 1990). Listen to the the sound of HU now at this Eckankar link: Experience the Sound of Soul: https://www.eckankar.org/experience/hu-the-sound-of-soul/
3) A free 5,000-word e-book called "Waking Dreams are Signs from the Universe" can be found on our blog. It defines waking dreams and cites examples of the various types and their uses. A second free e-book, "HU: An Ancient Mantra," can also be read or downloaded from the same page: https://signssynchronicityandwakingdreams.com/free-e-book/

Introduction

1) The etymology of the word god in English has been traced by linguists from Old English meaning "supreme being, deity" to Old High German *got* to both the Proto-Indo-European (PIE) root **gheu*—meaning "to pour" and to *ghut*—meaning "that which is invoked," which comes from **gheu(e)*— meaning "to call, invoke," which connects to Sanskrit *hūta*—"invoked," an epithet of the god, Indra, and *hŭ* meaning "calling a god by pouring an offering onto a fire," as described in the oldest San-

skrit text, the Rg-veda. Sources: (1) The entry "god" in *Etymology Online Dictionary*, www.etymonline.com, and (2) *Sanskrit-English Dictionary* by Monier Monier-Williams (Oxford: Clarendon Press, 1960), 1300-01 (*hŭ*), 1301 (*hūta*), and 1308 (*hve*).

PART I: CONNECTING WITH THE VOICE OF HU

Chapter 1: The Sanctuary of HU
1) Tr. by Kabir Helminsky, *Love is a Stranger* (Shambhala) 36-37.
2) Harold Klemp, *The Slow Burning Love of God,* Mahanta Transcripts, Book 13 (Minneapolis: Eckankar, 1996, 1997) 155.

Chapter 2: *A Cosmic Sea of Words*
1) Hazrat Khan, *The Sufi Message of Hazrat Inayat Khan, Book 2* (Barrie and Jenkins, London, 1962, 1973) 64.
2) See the column, "Sound," in Paul Twitchell's, "The God Worlds of ECK," *The Spiritual Notebook,* 1st ed. (Illuminated Way Press, 1971), 106-7.
3) Eckankar: The Path of Spiritual Freedom, https://www.eckankar.org
4) Claude Gruffy's website: http://www.claudegruffy.sitew.ca
5) Harold Klemp, *A Cosmic Sea of Words: The ECKANKAR Lexicon* (Minneapolis, Eckankar, 1998, 2nd ed.). This book defines many of the Eckankar terms with their proper pronunciation. It was replace by *ECKOPEDIA: The ECKANKAR Lexicon.*
6) Klemp, "Param Akshar," *Cosmic Sea of Words,* 152.
7) Klemp, "Voice of HU," *Cosmic Sea of Words,* 219.

Chapter 3: Dreams and the Dream Teacher
1) Carl Jung quote found on AZ Quotes: https://www.azquotes.com/quote/151484.
2) Harold Klemp, "Write It Down," *The Spiritual Exercises of ECK* (Minneapolis: Eckankar, 2nd ed. 1997, 3rd printing 2000) 163-4.
3) Klemp, "Door of Soul," *Spiritual Exercises of ECK*, 27.
4) Klemp, "Nirguna Ekam," *Cosmic Sea of Words*, 144-5.
5) Klemp, "Gopal Das," *Cosmic Sea of Words*, 84.

Chapter 4: Katsupari
1) Paul Twitchell, *ECKANKAR—The Key to Secret Worlds* (Minneapolis: Eckankar, 1969, 1987) 73.
2) Harold Klemp, *Those Wonderful ECK Masters* (Eckankar, 2005), 62. This book features eleven ECK Masters, their portraits, and easy-to-do spiritual exercises tailored to meet each of them. Colored pictures of these ECK Masters can be found on this website: https://www.eckankar.org/explore/spiritual-teachers/
3) Fubbi Quantz is one of the eleven ECK Masters featured in *Those Wonderful ECK Masters*, page 25; his colored picture is also included at https://www.eckankar.org/explore/spiritual-teachers/.
4) Paul Twitchell, *The ECK-VIDYA: Ancient Science of Prophecy* (Illuminated Way Press, 1972), 75-77. On page 13, Twitchell states, "The eighty-four on the wheel means the number of times we have births and deaths in the lower worlds. Eighty-four lacs amounts up to eight million, four hundred thousand times, for each lac equals one hundred thousand years. In other words, the individual Soul will go through each zodiac sign seven times in order to be able to conquer the influences outside Itself."

PART II: Solving Life's Challenges with HU

Chapter 5: Through the Doors of HU and Other Spiritual Exercises

1) Harold Klemp, "One with the HU," *The Sound of Soul* (Minneapolis: Eckankar, 2017) 63.
2) Masaru Emoto, "Saying 'Thank you' and 'You fool' to Rice Everyday," *Messages from Water,* Vol. 1 (HADO Publishing, ca.1990), 94.
3) Emoto, "Showing Letters to Water," *Messages from Water,* 96.
4) Klemp, "Show Me Love," *Spiritual Exercises of ECK,* 13.
5) Will Allen Dromgoole, "The Bridge Builder," first published in 1900.
   link:https://www.poetryfoundation.org/poems/52702/the-bridge-builder

Chapter 6: In Search of True North: Healing with HU

1) Louise L. Hay, *You Can Heal Your Life* (Hay House, 1984, 1987, 2004) 78.
2) Hay, *Heal Your Life,* (Diabetes, hypoglycemia) 164.
3) Klemp, "The Sound Room," *Spiritual Exercises of ECK,* 57.

Chapter 7: Opening the Heart with HU

1) Rumi, quote found on Goodreads: https://www.goodreads.com/quotes/9726-your-task-is-not-to-seek-for-love-but-merely
2) Klemp, "The Open Heart," *Spiritual Exercises of ECK*, 183.

Chapter 8: Being HU

1) Thich Nhat Hanh, quote found on Goodreads: https://www.goodreads.com/author/quotes/9074.Thich_Nhat_Hanh?page=4
2) Berthold Auerbach, German poet, https://www.brainyquote.com/authors/berthold-auerbach-quotes

PART III: THE UNIVERSE *Is* HU

Chapter 9: The Many Miracles of HU

1) Wayne Dyer quote found at https://www.azquotes.com/author/4269-Wayne_Dyer?p=4
2) Klemp, *Wonderful ECK Masters,* "Rebazar Tarzs," 92.
3) Klemp, "Calling upon the Little People," *Spiritual Exercises of ECK,* 73.
4) Harold Klemp, "Kay Meets Rami Nuri," *The Road to Spiritual Freedom,* Mahanta Transcripts, Book 17 (Minneapolis: Eckankar, 2016), 349-351.
5) Harold Klemp, "Teacher at a Temple of Golden Wisdom on Venus: Rami Nuri," *Wonderful ECK Masters,* 156.

Chapter 10: Animals Love HU, Too

1) Harold Klemp, "Charlie and Moon," *Animals are Soul too!* (Minneapolis: Eckankar, 1st edition, 2005; 2nd edition, 2023) 31.
2) "HU: Experience the Sound of Soul," Minneapolis: Eckankar, 2020). Posted on YouTube.

Chapter 11: Sharing the Gift of HU

1) Harold Klemp, *A Modern Prophet Answers Your Key Questions about Life, Book 3,* (Minneapolis: Eckankar, 2021), 151.
2) Rami Nuri and Kata Daki are featured in *Those Won-*

derful ECK Masters, pages 157 and 63 respectively; their colored pictures are also included at https://www.eckankar.org/explore/spiritual-teachers/

Chapter 12: Love Is a Never-ending Story
1) Rumi, quote found on Goodreads: https://www.goodreads.com/quotes/378568-wherever-you-are-and-whatever-you-do-be-in-love
2) The Eckankar Seat of Power was located in Sedona, Arizona, prior to moving to Chanhassen, Minnesota.

Epilogue: The Sound of Spiritual Freedom
1) Harold Klemp, "When Love Replaces Fear," *The Call of Soul* (Minneapolis: Eckankar, 2009) 83.

Acknowledgments
1) Sharon Sheppard communicates directly with pets and other animals. She can be contacted at (541) 574-1035, Pacific Time.
2) Claude Gruffy's website:
http://www.claudegruffy.sitew.ca.
3) Rose Elphick is a typesetter based in South Africa. email: dtpimpressions@mweb.co.za.

Michael Avery received a business degree from Linfield College in Oregon, where he also played shortstop on their 1971 National Championship baseball team. His post-college love of sports extended to Alpine skiing, tennis, and martial arts, earning a Black Belt in Tae Kwon Do.

Michael's love of writing began with poetry while living in Hawaii in his late twenties. He authored six children's picture books once back in the Pacific Northwest followed by *The Secret Language of Waking Dreams*, Michael's first book on spirituality. He has also written spiritual books under the pseudonym, Michael Harrington.

After a rewarding career as a water quality specialist, Michael retired and began writing full time. In 2021, he married Pichaya, who shares his love of writing, spirituality, animals, and nature.

Pichaya Avery composed twelve songs and played electric guitar in a popular band while attending high school in Kalasin, Thailand. She was also the band's lead singer. Pichaya majored in Linguistics and minored in Mass Communications at Ramkhamhaeng University.

Upon graduation, she worked for Thailand's largest bank prior to teaching English and serving as vice principal of a highly acclaimed bi-lingual school in Bangkok.

Pichaya moved to the U.S. in 1998. While living in California, she recruited American teachers for a bi-lingual school in Khon Khaen, Thailand, and worked as an interpreter at the Center for New Americans in Walnut Creek. After moving to Oregon, she became a Certified Life and Relationship Coach. Her former blog features insights on life, love, relationships, and personal growth.

In addition to raising three wonderful children, Pichaya's interests include, contemplation, spiritual growth, photography, playing the guitar, tennis, and walking in nature.

www.ingramcontent.com/pod-product-compliance
Lightning Source LLC
LaVergne TN
LVHW021714060526
838200LV00050B/2665